"Integration can be transformative not just for the organization, but for the people tasked with overseeing it. I certainly found that to be true, and my experience leading major integrations helped prepare me for the challenges of being CEO. In this book, David shares the many perspectives that we learned in collaboration together as consultant and client. From the big issues around people and culture to the finer details of synergy planning and tracking, he lights the way for leaders of all levels in this new go-to guide."

—**Robert Isom**, Chief Executive Officer, American Airlines

"*Post-merger Integration* underscores the 'client first' commitment that's made David such a dedicated and insightful advisor, and it's this commitment that makes the book so uniquely valuable. Rather than tell you what to do, he helps you make the decisions that best suit your circumstances while guiding you through the twists and turns. David has achieved a fresh approach to integration that will change how you think about attaining success."

—**Bob Gamgort**, Chairman and former CEO, Keurig Dr Pepper

"As a professor at Harvard Business School and Harvard Law School who teaches about deals and M&A, I rarely encounter a book that tackles post-merger integration with the clarity, practicality, and insight that David brings to this one. He distills the messy realities of integration into guidance leaders can actually use, offering remarkable clarity and wisdom along the way. It's an engaging, standout contribution that will elevate how executives and advisors approach integration."

—**Guhan Subramanian**, Joseph Flom Professor of Law & Business, Harvard Law School, Douglas Weaver Professor of Business Law, Harvard Business School

"In M&A, valuation, deal structuring, negotiation, and due diligence receive so much attention, but as David masterfully illustrates, the hard work is only beginning when the investment bankers wrap up. *Post-merger Integration* is essential reading for anyone serious about capturing deal value, not just announcing it."

—**Craig Oxman**, Vice Chairman with over 42 years of bulge bracket M&A and Investment Banking experience

"Working on integrations across my years at McKinsey and later as Head of Integration for one of the largest UK-listed software companies taught me that value is won or lost in the execution. David saw this long before it was fashionable, and he helped me see it too when I started working with him. This book brings together that insight, offering leaders the mindset and practical guidance to navigate the choices and tradeoffs that define successful integrations."

—**James McLetchie**, President and CEO, The Massy Group

POST-MERGER INTEGRATION

BUILDING THE MINDSET, SKILLS, AND DISCIPLINE NEEDED FOR DEAL SUCCESS

DAVID FUBINI

WITH PATRICK SANGUINETI

WILEY

Library of Congress Cataloging-in-Publication Data has been applied for:
ISBN 9781394380848 (Hardback)
ISBN 9781394380855 (ePub)
ISBN 9781394380862 (ePDF)

Cover Design: Wiley
Cover Image: © Nadezhda Fedorkova/Getty Images
Author Photos: Courtesy of the Authors
Printing and Binding: CPI Group (UK) Ltd, Croydon, CR0 4YY

C9781394380848_270426

For my wife Bertha and our four wonderful children:
Michael, William, Anna, and Marco

CONTENTS

ACKNOWLEDGMENTS

T his book is a project many years in the making, and there are many
I want to thank for their contributions and support in helping it
come to fruition.

My time with McKinsey & Company left an indelible mark on my life,
if this book is any indication. My consulting career coincided with a shift
in how we approach mergers and acquisitions (M&A) and post-merger
integration, and I will always be grateful for the firm's support in pursuing
a path that deviated from the norm. Of the hundreds of engagements that
inspired this work, each and every one was a team effort. This book is a
testament to the partnership of so many colleagues who made supporting
post-merger integration a collaborative and dynamic learning experience
unlike any other.

I am deeply grateful for the support of my colleagues at Harvard
Business School (HBS). As I approached my 35th year at McKinsey (my
"expiration date"), I had to face the unfamiliar reality of life beyond the
firm. It's hard to believe that was over a decade ago. It has been my honor to
collaborate with such an inspiring group of educators and thought leaders,

and my privilege to teach (and learn from) so many impassioned future leaders. In particular, I want to thank Guhan Subramanian and everyone who has participated in the Mergers and Acquisitions program for allowing me to share my experience and helping refine the thinking that eventually became this book.

My time at HBS has also allowed me to continue learning from countless leaders whose influence has helped shape this book for the better. Difficult as it is to single out just a few, I must thank Doug Parker, Elise Eberwein, and Robert Isom for their partnership in sharing the learnings from the US Airways–American Airlines merger with such a wide audience. I would also like to thank Bob Gamgort for sharing his time and wisdom with so many of my students. To the many other clients and leaders who have shared their stories, please accept my heartfelt thanks as well.

This book would not have been possible without the extraordinary contributions of Patrick Sanguineti. Patrick has been my collaborator in every sense of the word—an insightful researcher, a rigorous thinker, and a trusted partner in shaping not just this book, but much of the work we've undertaken together at HBS. His intellectual curiosity, analytical depth, and tireless commitment to clarity elevated every chapter and sharpened every argument. Patrick brings a rare combination of judgment, creativity, and discipline to his work, and his fingerprints are visible throughout these pages, as he has framed many of these ideas and helped shape the narrative throughout. I am deeply grateful for his partnership and for the joy of working alongside him on this and so many other HBS projects.

I also want to acknowledge Venkat Sankar, Judith Newlin, and the rest of the Wiley team for their efforts and support in getting this book across the finish line.

ABOUT THE AUTHOR

D avid G. Fubini is a Senior Lecturer and Henry B. Arthur Fellow in the Organizational Behavior Unit at Harvard Business School (HBS), where he also leads the Leading Professional Services Firm and Mergers & Acquisitions (M&A) executive education programs. Prior to academia, he was a Senior Partner of McKinsey & Company. Over his 35 years with the firm, David served as a Senior Partner, the co-founder and Managing Director of the Boston Office, the leader of the North American Organization Practice, and the co-founder and leader of the Worldwide Merger Integration Practice. In leading efforts for several dozen of the world's largest transactions and organizational turnaround efforts, he has helped clients architect and execute major transformational programs and witnessed major trends in M&A over three decades of deals.

A dedicated advisor, David has served as a member of numerous prominent corporate and civic boards. He is on the Board of Directors of Leidos, J. M. Huber, Bain Private Capital Board, and DLA Piper. He has previously been appointed as a Trustee of the University of Massachusetts, was named a member of the Massachusetts Court Management Advisory

Board, and was an Executive Committee member of the Boston Chamber of Commerce, the Boston Municipal Research Board, and the Inner City Scholarship Fund. He is also a member of the UMass Amherst Foundation and the UMass Eisenberg School of Business Dean's Committee. David formerly served as a member of the Shareholder Committee of ZS Associates Consulting, the Board of Compuware, and the HBS Dean's Advisory Council.

David is also the author of *Mergers: Leadership, Performance and Corporate Health* (2007); *Let Me Explain: Eugene G. Fubini's Life in Defense of America* (2009), a biography of his father's life; and *Hidden Truths: What Leaders Need to Hear but are Rarely Told* (2020). He has published articles on M&A in *Harvard Business Review*, including "Before a Merger, Consider Company Cultures Along with Financials" (2014), and has developed nearly 50 HBS case studies.

David received an MBA from HBS, with distinction, and a BBA from the University of Massachusetts, Amherst, with high honors.

INTRODUCTION

A MINDSET APPROACH TO POST-MERGER INTEGRATION

n the spring of 2024, members of Bain & Company's global M&A practice got together to reflect on the previous 20 years of deal development. Since the publication of their 2004 book, *Mastering the Merger*, things had drastically changed. We once lived in a paradoxical world where companies continued to pour billions and billions into transactional growth—think AOL–Time Warner, Daimler–Chrysler, even Mattel and The Learning Company—despite the understanding that anywhere between 70 and 90% of deals would fail to deliver expected value.[1] But in the span of a generation, that number has been flipped on its head, now with nearly 70% of deals succeeding and even more creating some degree of value.[2] Once synonymous with failure, M&A now represents an unavoidable—if not indispensable—fact of life for any company serious about growth.

How should we account for this change and why some deals still fail to return expected value? For years, many experts have focused on the risk of overpaying and the role of solid financial modeling in explaining failure.[3] Others have driven home the importance of strategic clarity and have pointed out that some companies mistake M&A for strategy, rather than an enabler of strategy.[4] Offering up their own explanation, the members of Bain's M&A practice reasonably noted that companies today are savvier at developing growth strategies, more sophisticated in carrying out due diligence, more serious about integration, and simply more experienced at doing deals,[5] perhaps suggesting that a lack in these areas could also account for coming up short.

While these are all valid ways to frame the picture, they're only so useful for leaders who want to lead their organizations to M&A success. Zooming out to the company or overall strategic level, for example, offers a sensible big-picture explanatory power, but it's less helpful for leaders who want to execute better deals or improve how they run integration but lack expertise in their organization, or want to apply more proven techniques. Meanwhile, zooming in to the concrete level of finance can provide a degree of empirical assuredness, but elevating it above all else risks treating M&A like a math problem that ignores the months of planning and labor needed to bring two companies together.

I've come to see the picture from a different angle. Over my 35 years at McKinsey & Company, and more than a decade at Harvard Business School, I've supported, worked with, and advised brilliant leaders who have both excelled at integration and made critical errors that cost their business. As we realized the victories and worked through the missteps, the picture gradually came into focus and now frames the arc of this book: **integration is what makes or breaks the success of a deal**. Not design, not financing, not due diligence, not negotiations of structure. Because no matter how expertly you handle these elements, if you can't bring all the pieces together, all your effort might as well have been an academic exercise. This, of course, raises the fundamental question: If integration determines deal success, then what's the best way to run it?

This book argues that the key to effective post-merger integration lies in mindset. After advising on nearly three dozen transactions of scale (including some of the largest in the world) and teaching about countless more, I've experienced many approaches to integration, and what connects every success is less a particular set of instructions and more the mentality of the leaders overseeing them. My goal is to help you achieve that mindset: rather than attempting (in vain) a single "best" model, this book is designed to help you formulate the model of "best fit" for your deal based on the nuances of your organization's circumstances.

MAKING THE CASE FOR A MINDSET APPROACH

Every deal is unique. As much as this might sound like the convenient kind of phrase an advisory firm would use to sell its services, it's the fundamental starting point when thinking about how to approach integration. Admittedly, it took me time to really appreciate it. The professional services industry selects for pattern recognition among its ranks, so as a consultant develops their experience from engagement to engagement, it's natural to start perceiving the echoes of similarity across different deals and bucketing them into "types." While trends do exist that become more visible with experience, anything that forces together two complex organisms will create the unpredictable: any change in variables, from the context to the terms, motivations, and more, can alter how things unfold to varying degrees of intensity.

To take this premise seriously, we also have to treat every integration as unique. If the specific combination of motivations, aspirations, players, industry, macro environment, and so on is individual, then how to take that combination and work toward the desired goal must be as well. That's why prescriptive how-to guides, generalized playbooks, and cookie-cutter frameworks so often fall short for integration: they may help with some specific processes or offer approaches that work under a particularly constrained set of circumstances, but they're not designed to help leaders figure out what they need and when they need it—which rarely remains constant from deal to deal.

By focusing on mindset, this book aims to enable you and your leaders to plan and implement the integration effort best suited to accomplish the goals you have for your deal. But in order for that to happen, it requires you to develop a precise answer to the following question: **Why are you doing the deal?** This isn't about what gets put in the public announcements—the *real* reasons are often too sensitive for wide disclosure so early. Instead, it's about discipline. While others have written about the risks of executives' lack of discipline in evaluating a deal's potential,[6] an integration mindset demands discipline in formulating the specific goals motivating the transaction. Only with this precise *deal rationale* will you be able to build and execute a successful integration plan. Without it, it's not just the advice in this book whose efficacy will be limited, but your organization's ability to capture intended value.

THE INTEGRATION MINDSET: NOT JUST FOR THE CEOs

What does this mindset look like in practice? Your thoughts might turn to big-name serial acquirers like Bob Iger, who jolted a Disney that had lost its way back to life with the acquisition of Pixar, and continued to expand the empire with blockbuster purchases of Marvel, Lucasfilm, and 21st Century Fox.[7] Or Satya Nadella, who increased Microsoft's value 10-fold in as many years on the back of major acquisitions like Minecraft's parent company Mojang, the professional networking site LinkedIn, the developer platform GitHub, the video game holding company ZeniMax Media, and the game publisher Activision Blizzard.[8]

But it's worth looking past the serial acquirers to isolate specific examples of leadership. Take Bob Gamgort and Olivier Goudet, for example, who had the strategic vision to formulate a merger between Keurig and Dr Pepper, whose rationale was based not around drink categories like coffee and soda, but around networks of distribution. Or Doug Parker, who was willing to make concessions that many acquirers wouldn't consider because it would allow him to realize the true reasons motivating US Airways' daring acquisition of the much larger American Airlines. Or Gary Saji and Takeshi Niinami, who exercised the patience and trust to allow Jim Beam management to take the lead in Suntory's global business as part of an integration learning process, before implementing their own best practices to vastly improve Beam's production.

And let's not limit ourselves just to the upper echelons of the CEOs and C-suite—in fact, this mindset is necessary for the hundreds of leaders whose work and buy-in are essential to run integration effectively. Whether tapped to join the Integration Management Office or support an Integration Team, whether they're a key functional leader put in charge of implementing vital integration plans or just assuming new responsibilities in the merged organization, this mindset is no less important for the Vice Presidents, Directors, Managers, and any number of other "rising stars" who will experience integration sometime in their career.

THIS BOOK'S APPROACH

This book's design emulates an advisor's approach to post-merger integration. On the one hand, it provides a foundational overview of an integration effort, walking you through its lifespan while covering the major decisions, considerations, processes, and roles that define each stage, from initial conception through implementation and future planning. But it also goes beyond the fundamental details in helping you determine the most critical set of decisions for your integration by introducing some of the different strategies you might employ, the options you might choose, and the tradeoffs you might face, as well as a selection of tested best practices, from a mixture of real-world experience and the academic and practitioner literatures. As a result, the book is organized largely chronologically across three thematic sections.

Part I focuses on how to frame an integration from its earliest inception. It starts by defining the mindset that's so crucial to integration leadership and success: in Chapter One, I'll discuss the traps that many integration efforts tend to fall into, as well as the "truths" that inform successful leaders' decision-making. Chapter Two is all about the players who will star in the effort, covering the specific roles, the criteria to optimize for in the selection process, and the organizational structure needed to keep those working on the integration effort and those responsible for the base business running smoothly in parallel. Chapter Three then addresses the major architectural design points that allow leaders to align the structure of the effort around their vision for the new organization.

Part II is all about integration planning and the early stages of the effort. Delving into the meat of the integration work, Chapter Four makes the case for detailed measuring and baselining, beyond any prior due diligence work, in developing a comprehensive, progress-oriented integration masterplan. Chapter Five covers communications: from a narrative framework to structure the entire communication effort to the various stakeholders that comprise your "audience," it addresses the many elements to plan for beyond the announcement. Rounding out the planning effort, Chapter Six flags what you need to ready as Day One looms—and how it's often much less than you think.

Part III covers the switch into the implementation. In Chapter Seven, I discuss how some elements of the effort wind down and others transition their responsibilities as the newly merged organization works toward implementing its integration goals while pursuing a new "business as usual." Chapter Eight offers a lens into one of the most challenging aspects of integration—cultural integration—through a phased approach that centers not on values, but on how work gets done. And in Chapter Nine, the conversation moves to completing integration: what winding down the effort entails, what "finished" looks like, and how to prepare for the next one.

Finally, in the Epilogue, I offer up some reflections from my experience as an integration advisor, both to pull back the curtain on what that work entails and how it shaped my own development, and to suggest how you might use integration to identify an advisor who can support you through so much more.

PART I

ENVISION: FRAMING THE INTEGRATION

CHAPTER ONE

BUILDING YOUR INTEGRATION MINDSET: THE TRAPS AND TRUTHS THAT UNITE EVERY DEAL

What separates a troubled integration from the most successful efforts? To help develop your integration mindset, I've distilled a series of lessons gathered over a vast array of deals. These lessons are divided into two sections: first, the leadership traps responsible for integration failure; and second, the truths that define effective integration leadership. These traps and truths are the foundational insights meant to prime your integration mindset, as well as the throughlines that will guide each of the chapters that follow. They are the starting point to help you steer your organization through the rough waters of integration—and to correct before you go too far off course.

THE TYPICAL TRAPS: WHY INTEGRATIONS TEND TO GO WRONG

I've never encountered a perfect integration, one where everything goes totally smoothly and according to plan. It's the nature of this endeavor: things will go wrong, markets will react, people will make mistakes. There's a lot that falls within acceptable parameters and is the understandable byproduct of an intense, strenuous undertaking. These are the kinds of challenges that any leader must handle in times of crisis and duress. This section is not about them.

Instead, this section is dedicated to the left tail of the bell curve: the endemic traps that snare unsuspecting (and perhaps overconfident) leaders. In my experience, an integration that fails to return anticipated value suffers from at least one of these traps. As a result, every responsible party, from the CEO down to the individual Integration Leaders, should be aware of them to spot the signs of an integration going awry.

The Copy–Paste Integration

M&A specialists are obsessed with typologies and look for them at every turn to break deals down into just the right boxes, in the hopes of understanding what makes them tick (and hopefully getting better future results). Academics are particularly guilty here: since at least the 1950s, researchers have been formulating deal typologies that fit broadly into two buckets (pre-acquisition strategies and integration variables), and while they can offer us interesting insight into the development of strategic management studies and the theoretical underpinnings of integration, they often fall short of answering the pragmatic questions that leaders are most interested in.[1] Figure 1.1, though somewhat dated, is one example of such a framework.

Figure 1.1   A classic example of an academic integration typology.

SOURCE: Adapted from Anthony Buono, *The Human Side of Mergers and Acquisitions: Managing Collisions Between People, Cultures, and Organizations* (San Francisco, CA: Jossey-Bass, 1989). Reprinted with permission of John Wiley & Sons, Inc.

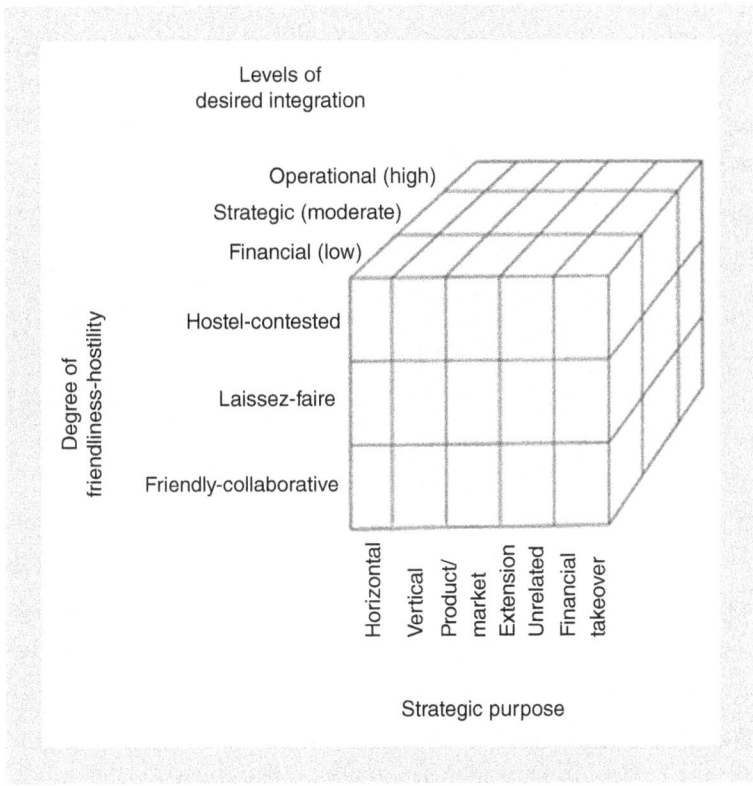

Consultants are no less guilty. When I was with McKinsey, we tried our hand at one that divided deals into six different "archetypes" based on the need of the acquirer to expand their current capabilities and the relative size of the acquired company, which acted as a matrix to inform our strategic recommendations along dozens of further "sub-types."[2] Every major firm has developed their own version based on their own unique experience with and approach to integration advising, the sum total of which represents a kaleidoscope of ways to analyze deals along minute lines of difference and similarity.

From the prevailing perspective, these kinds of categorizations are helpful because they visualize just how different deals can be, while also providing direction for the kind of integration approach that might best serve a certain sub-type. But over the years, I realized how limiting they really are. Beyond being hard to make sense of, they train us to think in boxes, which elides the most fundamental M&A truth: no two deals are the same—and neither are their integrations. Taking a copy–paste approach to integration based on existing or idealized models—no matter how precisely defined—invariably means a nuance gets overlooked and the reality of your effort starts going off script.

The Rationale Behind the Deal Falls Out of Sight

Every deal is done for a reason—or at least they should be, as I make the case for in this book. Developing a clear rationale contributes significantly to deal success. A 2024 Boston Consulting Group study found that, over the course of a decade, Asia Pacific deals exhibited a 5% higher rate of cancellation than the global average and the lowest share of reported synergies, in part due to a glaring dearth of strategic rationales: while 38% of Asia Pacific deals offered a clear and concrete rationale, 22% offered only a limited rationale (general statements and buzzwords over specific actions and impacts), and 40% provided no rationale. Those figures contrast sharply with North America and Europe, of whose deals 83 and 77%, respectively, produced clear rationales, and 17 and 23% offered limited rationales.[3]

But these strong numbers for North America and Europe conceal a second trap: formulating and/or announcing a clear rationale doesn't automatically translate to your ability to execute your integration around it. Countless times—particularly when public statements can't divulge the full extent of the underlying motivations—I've seen an organization lose sight of its deal rationale amid the immediate intensity and impending demands of integration. When this happens, your Newco loses valuable momentum and wanders after tangential interests before it can even get off the ground.

Efforts lose sight of the deal rationale often because they succumb to competing priorities, a critical factor that makes integration one of the most challenging kinds of transformation effort. Every level of your organization will be fighting to hit synergy targets while trying to keep up with their normal responsibilities, split duties that will be assessed according to distinct criteria. At the same time, the disruption triggered by the integration will impel business unit representatives to fight for changes that they believe will benefit themselves (and, they'll argue, the new business). After weeks spent wrangling with these competing priorities—operational and integration demands butting heads, visions of the future jockeying for favor—it's easy to veer from the critical path, even when that path had been clearly laid out.

The Pressure to Realize Target Synergies Creates Tunnel Vision

It's necessary to take a structured, dedicated approach to capturing the synergies you sketch out in your deal planning, whether cutting costs, growing revenues, taking advantage of new capital structures, or otherwise. But sometimes leaders are so determined to realize the synergy goals they had envisioned that they don't allow themselves to consider new options that emerge only once integration has begun. Or they find themselves tenaciously pursuing synergies that made sense during strategic planning but don't work as well once all the details of the acquired company come to light. In the end, they fail to take advantage of the true potential of their deal by leaving value on the table, or even risk squandering the value they had planned for by failing to adapt to changing conditions. In either case, they keep their lens too narrow.

Both kinds of tunnel vision are the result of a risk-avoidance mindset that clings too tightly to due diligence projections. This might sound strange—after all, conducting thorough due diligence and minimizing risk on the buy side of the transaction are vital to securing overall deal success. But the truth is that due diligence, even when thorough, often doesn't fully reflect the post-close reality: as my former McKinsey colleagues James McLetchie and Andy West found, in nearly half of the 83 deals they studied, due diligence proved inaccurate and ultimately "failed to provide an adequate roadmap for capturing synergies and creating value."[4] In many of these cases, they found that the Integration Teams played it too conservatively by focusing tightly on running the process they had already laid out, only coming back up from under the water when it was too late.

The Base Business Loses Focus—and Momentum

The 2002 merger between Hewlett-Packard (HP) and Compaq often ranks among the most troubled transactions in M&A history—something to which I can attest, having been brought in as part of the consulting team two weeks before the announcement. Some of the headline items will sound familiar if you were around at the time. As the first HP CEO to be brought in from the outside, Carly Fiorina was determined to shake things up.[5] In a way, she did: Walter Hewlett, son of HP's founder and then a director for the company, vehemently protested the proposal, ostensibly out of concern that the deal would dilute HP's successful printer business,[6] and his protest sparked a months-long legal battle that not only pushed the integration back six months,[7] but also forced the redevelopment of the entire integration plan, and even resulted in the callback and subsequent surprise departure of former Compaq CEO Michael Capellas.[8]

To say that people on both sides of the deal were distracted would be a gross understatement. And that's not even considering the broader context: the deal was announced just after the collapse of the dot-com bubble, which sent some of the companies' partners into a "state of panic,"[9] and only a week before the September 11 attacks and the start of the war in Afghanistan.

All of these distractions enacted a considerable toll through the integration. The internal dynamics severely impacted the integration planning and execution, resulting in billions in restructuring costs and related expenses, while the gravitational pull toward the integration also catalyzed a loss of $2 billion in revenue in the immediate post-merger quarter.[10] Though one of the most extreme cases, HP–Compaq showed how damaging losing focus on the base business can be, as well as the added difficulty that lost momentum imparts on achieving deal success.

Earlier, I described integration as a challenge of competing priorities, and the most significant of those is the struggle between synergy goals and the base business. Now, it's not really these two things themselves that are competing: the base business is the engine keeping your organization moving forward, meaning that all future-oriented integration efforts are really building off this engine, and that any amount of steam lost by that base business engine will necessarily cap how much synergy value you're able to capture. Instead, the competition is between *the amount of attention* given to each of them. Focusing too singularly on synergy capture risks disrupting existing business momentum, and when this happens, companies typically experience the "year-one dip," a decline in revenue over the first year of the integration that most successful integrations avoid.[11]

The difficulty—the real reason for the competition—is that 99% of your team working on the integration will only be doing so on a part-time basis. Aside from the small number of full-time members staffed on the Integration Management Office (IMO), everyone else will be splitting their time between their day jobs (the base business) and their relevant portion of the integration effort. In other words, an Integration Leader in sales will be expected to demonstrate progress toward synergy goals while still maintaining standard performance. Empowering these Integration Leaders to do so starts with truly dedicated and informed leadership from the top down.

The Acquired Company Gets All the Scrutiny and Attention

A "merger of equals" is rarely, if ever, equal. Even in a cashless merger, where companies can avoid the awkward business of one visibly buying the other, you still have to decide who's in charge, what everyone's titles will be, what benefits you offer—consequential quality-of-life factors that say a lot about the real balance between two supposed equals.[12] The practical truth is that any deal will involve a power imbalance where one side gets more say. When US Airways merged with the much larger American Airlines, the company kept the American Airlines name, systems, even the Dallas headquarters, but it was the US Airways leadership under CEO Doug Parker calling the shots.

The imbalance in power naturally leads to an imbalance in focus during integration. The acquirer (the decision-maker) has so much to learn about its newly acquired partner and very little time. What's the true state of their assets? What's their secret sauce, and how do we fold that into our operation? Who do we want to let go, and how do we keep the people we want the most? Faced with an entire organization of unknowns, the acquiring leaders will dedicate much more scrutiny to the acquired side than to their own.

But acquirers that do this risk missing out on transformational synergies from within their organization, and even risk harming their own business in the process. Every organization has inefficiencies or redundancies that can be improved through a merger, provided that the acquirer is willing to take a good, hard look at itself and assess all the available options according to first principles. Far less appreciated, however, is the anxiety among the employees of the acquiring side, thousands of whom are wondering what all this means for them. Not addressing their concerns and instead directing all the attention toward bringing the acquired employees into the fold can hamper base business momentum in ways that many leaders don't realize.

Your Decision-Making Relies Too Much on Data—or Too Much on Gut

This isn't meant to sound vexing or vague. But the apparent double bind of its framing reflects the exasperation so many unprepared leaders face as they work their way through integration. Without a doubt, this trap is the hardest for the majority to overcome because it works counter to two of today's most ingrained decision-making tendencies. And it proves especially fatal: over my career, I have found that the success of the transaction depends as much (or even more) on the implementation as the conception, but that the ability to implement effectively depends first on decisive, rationale-based decision-making during the planning stage.

Before I go further, a word on the categorical challenge of integration planning leadership: *time*. You just don't have much of it. Compounding the scarcity of time is the sequential, cascading nature of the imminent decision tree, starting with your top leaders and deal architecture and working on down. Taken together, you're left with little option but to execute swiftly, lest you risk stumbling out of the gate.

This is a problem for most leaders who, according to a 2019 McKinsey survey, spend nearly 40% of their time making decisions.[13] Michael Porter and Nitin Nohria's enlightening study of how CEOs spend their time only underscores this point: they urge chief executives to strike a savvy balance between direct decision-making and pulling informal levers given the innumerable holds on their schedule.[14] And that's under normal circumstances, without the added integration demands.

And though any good leader will have experience operating under time pressure, few are comfortable simultaneously operating under low confidence. Compared to those I served on my earliest engagements, today's leaders undoubtedly leverage data to a far greater degree. Following the advent of machine learning and increasingly robust analytical tools, we're well within a paradigm of data-driven decision-making, a term that has become accepted enough to earn its own acronym (DDDM). DDDM is all about increasing the efficacy of an organization's decision-making by generating insights from diverse data sets that leaders can act on. It's about enhancing—though some might go as far as to say *replacing*—gut intuition. And setting aside the biases that can be baked into analytical models, most would agree that the DDDM paradigm has significantly improved decision-making by increasing confidence in available options.[15]

Integration makes this kind of decision-making extremely difficult. Especially during the compressed planning window, you won't have immediate access to the data you'd want to shore up your confidence levels. It will be tucked away in an organization you're unfamiliar with, through channels you haven't yet established, among an entire business-worth of other data points that your systems might not even be able to read. By the time you sort through it all to build the confidence you're used to, it's already too late—you've missed your window of opportunity.

The other side of this balance also presents issues, much to the same refrain as the second trap above. For that reason, I'll keep it short: overconfidence in gut feel can also hamper deal success. Rather than waiting too long on data to confirm their directions, some leaders are so trusting of the process (or the sense of similarity with those on the other side of the negotiating table) that they fail to rigorously test every decision against the deal rationale or simply don't act with enough urgency. In recent years, I've found this to be less and less common, as the majority of dealmakers are aware of the difficulty of the endeavor. All the same, false confidence can easily creep in when both merging companies seem alike, a dangerous dynamic I examine more in Chapter Eight.

UNIFYING TRUTHS: STEPS TOWARD BUILDING AN INTEGRATION MINDSET

In my privileged years working with excellent leaders, I've also seen many successful ways to run integration. The contexts could vary drastically—from airlines to beverages, pharmaceuticals, mining, and more—and the nuances of the integrations did too, but there were a few first principles that ran through all of them and contributed to their success. While it's difficult to abide by all of them, they are true of every integration I've considered the most effective.

These truths don't map one-to-one onto the traps above—it's not that the first directly responds to the first, the second to the second, and so on. But cumulatively, they provide the way not just to avoid the traps, but to chart a bespoke path to integration success. Ordered roughly in an accretional way, where each subsequent truth builds on its predecessor, they are the aggregated qualities that all Integration Leaders should embody.

Always Keep the Deal Rationale Central

Why did you do the deal? That's the question that you, your lieutenants, and your advisors should be asking at every step of the integration, from initial planning all the way through final execution. The answer to that question is your *deal rationale*, and it is the answer that should anchor each and every one of your decisions.

A strong deal rationale is concrete and testable. It provides a specific reason (or set of reasons) behind your acquisition that you can work toward through integration, such that, if everything goes according to plan, it can be firmly proven or disproven by the time both companies are fully integrated. It is, to borrow a term that's popular in private equity and venture capital circles, an investment thesis, a statement "that outlines how adding this particular business to your portfolio will make your company more valuable."[16] Or, in even simpler terms, something that "tells me why I would want to own this business."[17] It is the specific way you intend to use the transaction to achieve your company's broader strategic goals, how you will translate the deal into "an important enabler of strategy and long-term value."[18]

There are a few ways you can formulate this rationale (or thesis, or hypothesis) to increase your odds for overall success. In the simplest terms, "We're acquiring *x company* for *y reason* in order to grow." Or, "By acquiring *x company*, we can leverage *a, b, and c assets* to grow *in y ways.*" Alternatively, leaning into the hypothesis formulation, "If we acquire *x company*, then..." or, "We believe that, by acquiring *x company*, we will..." But in each of these framings, providing the specific reason(s) is absolutely required. A solid deal rationale is *not*, "We will acquire *x company* in order to grow," full stop.

Let's get specific by returning to three of the leaders mentioned in the Introduction. For Doug Parker, CEO of US Airways, the rationale was all about scale: by acquiring American Airlines, he could get the systems and facilities needed to make his company a global airline. Bob Gamgort, CEO of the coffee maker Keurig Green Mountain, realized that, by acquiring Dr Pepper Snapple, the combined company could leverage Pepper's powerful direct-store-deliver network to drastically increase the distribution of its brands. Gary Saji and Takeshi Niinami, Chairman and President/CEO of the Japanese brewing and distilling group Suntory, bet that acquiring and integrating Beam Inc. would give them not only a foot in the

US market, but also new leadership partners who could transform Suntory from a predominantly Japanese company into a truly global enterprise.

In each of these cases, the deal rationale dictated every turn of their respective integrations. This was the first major reason behind the success of their deals overall, and it was something they were able to accomplish through dedicated integration planning.

Integration Planning: Translating the Deal Rationale into Action

Integration planning is where you take the rationale behind your deal and develop the steps your organization will need to prove it out. Chapters Four through Six are all about the specifics of integration planning, so for now, I want to describe at a high level what sets it apart from other kinds of planning, including types you will have done earlier in the deal process.

If you're prepping for a merger, you've most likely already been doing a lot of planning. It's possible you've spent a year or even longer developing a sound corporate strategy, identifying a promising deal target, drafting up the anticipated synergies as part of the strategic plan, doing the due diligence, hearing from the investment bankers about how much value this should create, and perhaps, after all that work and planning, you've even (finally!) consummated the deal. This is already a significant endeavor. In fact, it's so significant that it leads many leaders to confidently think that the right mix of compelling vision, advice from outside counsel, and inspirational communication will make the rest come together. Unfortunately, this point is not a climactic finale with a neat postscript to come. Instead, it's the transition from strategic planning to the dedicated planning needed to launch the integration.

Strategic planning and integration planning represent distinct processes, but they are interconnected. The strategic plan sketches the goals for the deal in big-picture terms. The integration plan, meanwhile, lays out the path to accomplishing those goals (the deal rationale) in specific, granular detail. Though what goes into integration planning will change according to the nature of the deal, the integration plan is fundamentally built out of the deal rationale so that the new organization can realize the strategic goals intended for the deal.

These two planning efforts differ in their degree of granularity. Strategic planning is necessarily a high-level sketch because of the limitations of due diligence: without full access to the acquired company, the planners on the acquiring side are producing more of a "best guess" to be proven—or tweaked, or even disproven—once more data is available.

Integration planning must be much more granular, specific, and comprehensive for it to be actionable. It's also an iterative process of refining as the effort progresses. In practice, a strategic plan might sketch the framework for what the deal hopes to accomplish with about 20 lines of detail, while the integration plan must cover every decision point—large, medium, and small—with upwards of a thousand lines.

Think of this portion of the deal process like product testing. The strategic plan is the conceptual design that outlines the vision: it sketches out how the new product will be faster, lighter, and more agile than what came before. The integration plan, meanwhile, comprises the blueprint for each individual element, how they will fit together, and even which pieces of the old model get jettisoned, and how. Chances are that the first version of this plan will need adjusting: as you roll out the initial prototype, maybe some features aren't working as intended, and perhaps some of the things you thought would be important can be done without or saved for later. As you iterate and learn, you continually update your plan until you achieve the right balance.

The integration plan thus sets out to accomplish the goals outlined by the broad strategic plan in actionable, iterative fashion. Unlike the strategic plan, it will naturally evolve over the course of the effort as you continue to learn and implement decisions. This may feel like a voyage of discovery, because even with rigorous due diligence, you'll almost certainly find yourself uncovering unexpected opportunities (and problems) along the way—which, as it turns out, is a vital part of the process.

Embrace the Uncertainty Principle: There's a Lot That You Won't Know—and Won't Be Able to Know

How do you make decisions as a leader? How do you inform your judgment? Chances are you've trained yourself to rely on analytics, or maybe you've developed an efficient model internal to your organization that allows you to make informed decisions with confidence. But these high-confidence approaches to decision-making, almost taken for granted in today's world, don't work for integration planning, where time is critically short and meaningful data is difficult to access.

The leaders who are most adept at integration planning are those who internalize what I call the Uncertainty Principle. They recognize the tradeoff between a rapidly closing decision-making window and the desire to make an informed decision, and they understand that the former puts a hard cap on the latter. They're quick to seek out informed opinions only from those closest to the relevant issue, and they aren't afraid to set the direction according to the deal rationale they formulated. In the end, they know they'll have to make decisions with only a 70% confidence level, so they let their hunches guide them in reaching a minimum viable direction that can be tweaked down the road, if needed.

This medium-confidence decision-making is very hard because it forces you to rely more on your own judgment than external sources of validation. The traditional approach to developing sound judgment involves active and attentive listening, seeking out diverse perspectives (to confirm, deny, or refine your hypotheses), thoroughly questioning the solutions offered to you, and balancing short- and long-term ramifications.[19] And while these principles still hold true, when you have dozens of critical decisions to make (many of which are co-dependent) in only a few days' time, you can only rely on them so much. You might just have to trust in what has gotten you this far in your career: as my HBS colleague Reza Satchu argues around his notion of the "founder mindset," judgment is a muscle that you build with reps—by decisively making more decisions of consequence.[20]

Pay Attention to Both the Acquired and Acquiring Companies

Sandwiched between George W. Bush's second presidential inauguration and Super Bowl XXXIX, there came major M&A news: two personal care giants were joining forces. Gillette, the men's razor company based out of Boston, had come to terms with Procter & Gamble (P&G) in a deal that would transform P&G from the largest packaged goods company in the United States to the largest worldwide. Although headlines stated the significantly larger P&G was buying Gillette in an acquisition worth $57 billion,[21] the two sides adamantly declared the deal a merger. Their intent to make this a reality emerged as integration planning unfolded. One week before Gillette announced its senior management appointments, a memo unveiled a plan to "field the best team" from members of both organizations.[22] With this one update, internal impressions changed drastically: Gillette employees now felt like they had a shot at staying with the company, while P&Gers realized they might be on the chopping block.

Among the many lessons this deal has for us, P&G and Gillette underscore the importance of paying attention to both sides in integration planning and execution. Setting aside the premise behind "field the best team," the dynamics that emerged in its wake remind us how strongly people respond to the uncertainties of a merger. Integration studies often emphasize how difficult it can be for acquired employees: a 2024 study by Wharton's J. Daniel Kim, for example, has shown that roughly 33% of acquired workers left within the first year of an acquisition in the startup context.[23] But employees in the acquiring company are largely taken for granted, as if they aren't also wondering about how their organization will change, even if their employment status isn't explicitly at risk.

Effective integrations take into account both sides of the emerging Newco. Maintaining base business momentum, let alone creating a cohesive whole from two once-separate parts (who may have been long-time competitors not too long before), requires careful attention toward all employees, which includes tailored messaging and dedicated resources. In so doing, leaders demonstrate a continued commitment to the people whose work contributed to their company's position as an acquirer, just as they're concerned with smoothly bringing a new group of people into the fold. And its benefits aren't limited to preventing stagnation—it also helps you identify unforeseen opportunities that increase the value potential of your deal.

"Unfreezing" Your Organization: The Hunt for Transformational Synergies

"Our people, our customers and the communities we serve around the world have been anticipating the arrival of the new American. We are taking the *best of both* US Airways and American Airlines to create a formidable competitor, better positioned to deliver for all of our stakeholders" (emphasis mine).[24] This announcement by CEO Doug Parker, which signaled from the outset a commitment to a "best of both" approach, sounds awfully similar to Gillette and P&G's integration. Now, for reasons I'll cover in Chapters Three and Five, explicitly adopting a "best of both" approach to integration—let alone announcing it publicly—isn't something I advise unless the deal rationale clearly justifies it. But through this commitment, both integrations demonstrate the transformational value that can come from taking a close look not just at the acquired organization, but at the acquiring organization as well.

First, we need to talk about synergies. Derived from the Ancient Greek meaning "to work together," synergies are positive, value-generating outcomes from combining capabilities, and are thus tangible measures of integration success. They come in a few different forms, the three most basic being cost (savings from, e.g., staff reductions), revenue (increases in, e.g., sales), and financial or capital (benefits from, e.g., increased cashflow).[25] But we can also bucket synergies based on how we expect to find them and the second-order ways in which they create value: combinational synergies are the typical cost and capital opportunities that planners build anticipated deal value around, while transformational synergies are unexpected value generators that emerge only after careful scrutiny of both companies and creative thinking on how to make changes going forward.[26] Figure 1.2 offers a simple breakdown.

By closely comparing the relationship that each company had with its channel partners, P&G was able to transform its go-to-market. Initial hopes behind the deal centered on revenue synergies: by joining forces,

Figure 1.2   Types of synergies.

Synergy Type	Cost	Revenue	Capital (Balance Sheet)
Combinational	• Eliminating redundancies (e.g., staffing overlaps) • Economies of scale (e.g., supply chain efficiencies)	• Cross selling / complementary products • Complementary geographies	• Real estate leases • Design of foreign tax subsidiaries
Transformational	• Renegotiating partner relationships • Outsourcing opportunities	• New go-to-market / market opportunities	• Supply chain (e.g., minimizing tariffs, regulatory taxes)

these contenders in men's and women's care could control more shelf space and maybe put their best and brightest together to create new products. But as the Integration Teams got underway, they came to a promising realization. Since they operated in similar product spaces, the two companies shared many of the same partners—only Gillette had been able to negotiate better deals with many of them. P&G took the opportunity to use Gillette's contracts as the model going forward, a transformational discovery that produced significant savings for the combined company—and started with a hard look in the mirror.

For American Airlines and US Airways, transformation came at multiple levels. It's easy to point to the many ways in which US Airways (the acquirer, despite being smaller) looked at its own systems and decided instead to adopt swaths of American Airlines' in order to become truly global. But I think a more telling example is that of the old Pittsburgh training facility. For years, US Airways had maintained this facility as a relic from its days as Allegheny Airlines pre-1979. It meant a lot to a regional group who had been with the airline through decades of turbulence, and though it became steadily less practical as US Airways flew further and further away from its bygone self toward national and international scale, its history made it untouchable. Any attempt to phase it out resulted in unresolvable debate that pitted organizational identity against practicality. But with all the cards laid out during integration planning, a new kind of opportunity emerged: American Airlines had a huge training facility in Dallas, much better suited to the needs of the soon-to-be massive, combined organization. And with the decision to adopt American Airlines' Dallas headquarters, US Airways' leaders could finally pull the trigger. They phased out the old facility.

In both of these cases, the acquirers took advantage of a brief window of organizational "unfreezing" during integration to reshape themselves in ways transformational yet unanticipated prior to the deal. The term harkens to a model of organizational change attributed to the pre-eminent social psychologist Kurt Lewin, which holds that any successful change process involves at least three basic steps: unfreezing (identifying a habit, behavior, etc., and resolving to change it), moving (working to change it), and (re)freezing (working to solidify and cement the changed behavior).[27] As a quintessential example of organizational change, integration is the perfect opportunity for the acquirer to look carefully at itself and ask, "What can we do better? And in which of those areas can our newly acquired partner help?"

Effective integrators are primed to take advantage of the unfreezing window to identify new possibilities that can only come to light during dedicated planning. They're also ready to do so decisively, given how little time there is for integration planning before implementation, and how unlikely it is to find new opportunities once the entire organization is focused on carrying out the established plan.[28] They let the deal rationale guide the hunt rather than a boil-the-ocean approach, and they're willing to scrutinize the way their organization has come to do things in the spirit of driving true transformational change beyond what was initially scoped for the deal.

Measure for Success, Measure to Correct

In a 2020 episode of *Inside the Strategy Room*, a podcast that spotlights McKinsey insights, Senior Partner Andy West, joined by Partner Jeff Rudnicki, discussed the challenges, concerns, and misconceptions that their clients had around synergies and value creation through M&A. Their comments touched on many of the same issues I encountered throughout my career: not maintaining the base business, thinking mostly of traditional combinational rather than transformational synergies, setting too conservative targets for Integration Teams to shoot for.[29] Their remarks reveal not only *that* leaders continue to lose sleep over synergy capture, but also *how many ways* they seem to be missing the mark.

If you want to untangle the reasons why a deal might fail to create anticipated value, you might as well be untying the Gordian knot. From valuation through to integration implementation, there are countless perspectives and analyses that influence your targets' creation, just as there are countless hands that shape progress toward their realization. Instead, I've found that truly effective leaders are interested more in cutting the proverbial knot altogether. Though they're still curious about how things might deviate from expectation, they train their efforts on how they can track progress and intervene if necessary.

The key is something so simple that it's surprisingly often overlooked: measuring. This might be particularly surprising given how data-centric our world has become, where it feels like every minuscule data point can be mined and analyzed in pursuit of some broader takeaway. But effective measuring requires commitment to a process that some leaders lose track of when their sight is fixed on the synergy pie in the sky that emerged from deal planning. This process spans the entire integration: it tells you your starting point, tracks your progress toward your target goal, and conveys whether that target goal is actually feasible. It's even what allows you to determine if the synergies you planned are really worth pursuing, because there's a cost to achieve each one—what Deloitte's Mark Sirower and Jeffery Weirens call the "synergy-matching principle"[30]—and sometimes that cost outweighs the value you hope to produce.

It's in this measuring context during integration implementation that DDDM can play a vital role. Although integration planning will push you toward medium-confidence decision-making, data analytics and technology make tracking progress toward synergy goals much more transparent, and they can even speed the realization of those goals along a quicker timeline (though in every case, you need to be very clear about *what* it is you're measuring).[31]

From establishing robust baselines to setting regular tracking cadences, evaluating progress, and determining the need for change, effective leaders commit themselves to measuring. It's a commitment whose absence once formed a warning: If you don't measure it, it won't change. But over time, as I saw the transformative potential of such a fundamental process, it gradually grew into a more positive mantra that all leaders should recite: If you measure it, change will come.

Commit to the Parallel Process: Run Integration Activities and Management Decision-Making Separately

Throughout this chapter, "base business" has made a few appearances that paint a concerning picture: it's something that's easy to lose track of during integration, and if it loses focus, it's bound to hinder success. What should you do to keep up momentum and concentrate efforts on both the integration and base business? The answer, I've found, lies in how rigorously you construct your chains of command.

Effective leaders abide by what I call the Parallel Process. It starts with empowering the IMO as *the* go-to authority on all integration matters. While ultimate decision-making rests with the CEO, the IMO oversees the activities of the individual Integration Teams and is deputized as the buffer between business unit/functional leaders and the chief executive on integration matters. This structure clearly delineates who is responsible for making integration decisions versus business-as-usual decisions—a model without which Integration Leaders, already torn between dual responsibilities, can easily lose their footing.

Enforcing the Parallel Process comes with its obstacles. Trusted functional heads, intentionally left off the integration to maintain their vital roles, may want to challenge the IMO on decisions concerning their fiefdoms. But permitting end-runs undercuts the IMO when their leadership is most needed, threatens to take the integration in directions off the critical path, and puts Integration Leaders in an even thornier position in making sense of whose direction they're supposed to follow. By separating integration and base business decisions across parallel pathways, you keep the right people's focus on the right places, securing base business momentum and minimizing attention lost in navigating needlessly complex lines of authority.

THE WAY FORWARD: TRANSLATING TRUTHS INTO ACTION

Of course, it's not enough just to know the truths behind effective integration. As Stanford's Jeffrey Pfeffer and Robert Sutton keenly observed nearly three decades ago, there's a significant gap between knowing and doing that we're so prone to fall into.[32] That's why I've dedicated the remainder of this book to the contexts and ways you can implement the elements of the Integration Mindset I've introduced above. And though you won't find many prescriptions—all integrations are bespoke, after all—you will find the insights and tools you'll need to get that much closer from knowing about successful integration to actually doing it. Let's get started.

CHAPTER TWO

FIELDING YOUR TEAM: ESSENTIAL INTEGRATION ROLES AND THE RIGHT PEOPLE TO PLAY THEM

The Michael Jordan Bulls were famous for it. From Spielberg to Kubrick and Fincher, they've all been praised for it. Even at a wedding reception before the speeches and choreographed dances, we come to expect it. The starting lineup, the opening credits, the party's introductions. Across so many facets of our culture, we expect to know who will be playing the central roles before the big event.

With an undertaking as big as integration, it should be no different. But unless they have good counsel or they've been through it before, leaders often only have a vague sense of the players involved, when it's a much more detailed understanding they'll need to staff such a major effort. Whether it's the Steering Committee, the IMO, or the individual Integration Teams, every leader must know how the teams fit together and what roles they need to play—and this chapter addresses just that. But more than a roll call, this chapter will also introduce you to the bespoke challenges each role will face and provide advice on the criteria for picking the appropriate candidates. Critically, this chapter also frames these roles in the context of the Parallel Process, the separation of base business and integration decision-making that's essential for effective planning and implementation. By the end, you'll have a clear sense of the staffs you'll need for integration success, as well as the structure that senior leaders will need to supply to keep the integration—and the base business—managed smoothly.

PRIMING THE PARALLEL PROCESS: YOUR DUAL CHAINS OF COMMAND

Staffing represents one of a multitude of obstacles endemic to integration. More than who will fill each role and what qualifications they'll need, leaders must think carefully about how they allocate their organization's resources and how to enforce new divisions of authority and responsibility. Although integration will touch everyone in the organization, only a few will work on it full time, while the majority of the process will rely on staff splitting their time between integration and their regular responsibilities. This is by necessity, as few businesses can afford to "lose" so many talented employees to the integration effort: even if they're still contributing significantly to the overall organization, they must also keep up their core operational responsibilities at the same time.

These split responsibilities raise important questions. If the part-time Integration Team members are expected to report to both the IMO and their functional leader, how are they supposed to navigate their dual obligations? How is the IMO supposed to wield authority when their support staff are essentially part-time? And what can be done to keep the experienced operational leaders left in charge of the base business sufficiently focused on their core responsibilities, despite the vortex pull of the integration effort and its implications for their business unit?

Solving these quandaries requires a systemic solution: a dual leadership structure. By separating base business management from integration decision-making, you enable continued operational efficiency while empowering those working on the integration to plan and execute according to the priorities they identify, without undue intervention. This is the first step of what I refer to as the Parallel Process. With consistent reinforcement by senior leadership, these dual chains of command create a reporting structure that bolsters the authority of the IMO and erects enforceable barriers to keep base business leaders focused on their key responsibilities.

Figure 2.1 provides a simplified version of the Parallel Process structure. Please note that this structure pertains only to the integration planning phase prior to Day One, the day when both companies are legally made a combined entity. While Chapters Six and Seven will cover the nuances of planning for and implementing post-Day One, for this discussion, know that legal close will allow you to start putting together an integrated corporate structure, and that the start of the implementation phase from Day One will mark the end of the Integration Teams' part-time integration work.

The left side of the figure represents the base business or "business as usual" chain. This side keeps things going as they were before the deal: both the acquiring and the acquired companies maintain their respective senior/executive leadership teams, who continue to oversee the respective businesses as they had pre-deal. The decision-making here is formally separate from the integration work handled by the right side of the figure. The one exception is the CEO: since the acquiring CEO almost always becomes the CEO of the combined company, they will naturally contribute to both their company's base business and the combined integration planning.

Figure 2.1   The dual chains of command.

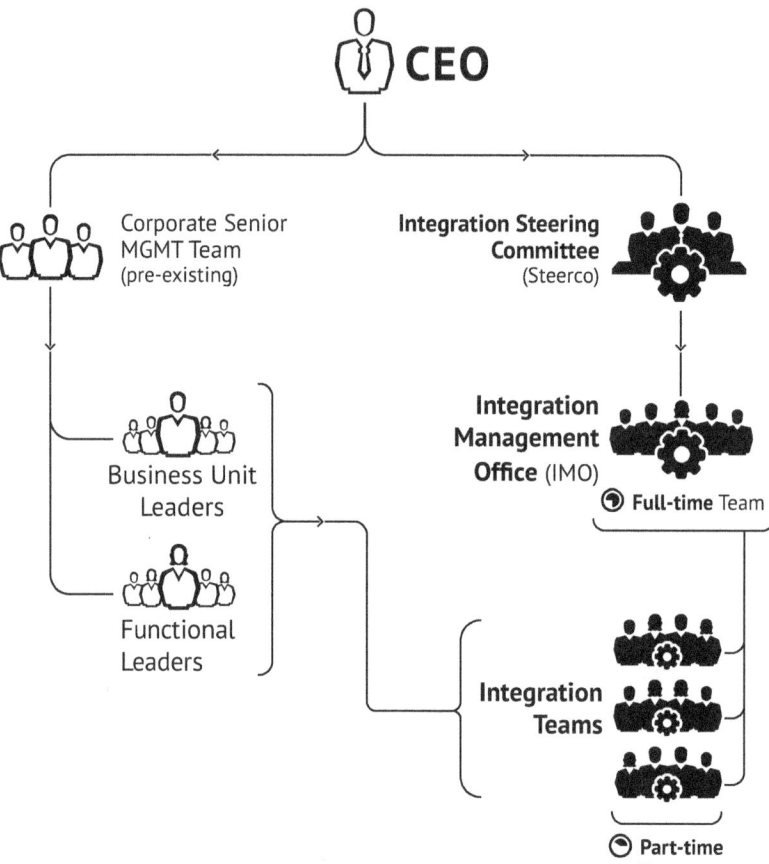

Nevertheless, as much as possible, the base business leadership must strive to keep on as things were to maintain momentum vital for the integration's success.

The right side of the figure comprises the integration chain. The members of this select group—from the senior leaders in Steerco, to the IMO responsible for project management, to the individual Integration Teams—must operate as if independent of the base business chains ("as if" because, after all, members of Steerco and the part-time Integration Teams also have their "day jobs" running parts of the base businesses). That critically involves mindset: Steerco and the IMO will especially need to embrace the Uncertainty Principle and make decisions with only a 70% confidence level, but with a high certainty of impenetrability, unlike the base business leaders, who operate with far greater certainty.

The separation that's needed between the two chains, however, is hard to maintain, in no small part because only the IMO will be working full time on the integration. The members of the Integration Teams may have a particularly difficult time, given that, as part-time contributors to the integration effort, they will have to juggle these new demands with their existing base business responsibilities (see the lines of oversight from the Business Unit and Functional Leaders in the figure). This challenge makes a formally separate hierarchy all the more necessary, so that any potential conflict can be resolved in the interest of the integration.

The makeup of these teams and their areas of focus will vary according to your deal's rationale and, as Chapter Three will address, the integration architecture that Steerco decides upon accordingly. Figure 2.2 on the next page, shows what a prototypical integration chain might look like, including how the responsibilities might be divvied up.

Why the Parallel Process? A Cautionary Tale

While planning for a major integration, the acquiring CEO contemplated how to structure his Steerco. This CEO trusted deeply in his full management team and felt that their input would best serve the new organization early and throughout the planning stage. Rather than draw up a separate Steerco, he decided to fold integration matters into the regular senior management meetings each week, setting aside an additional 30 minutes on top of their existing two-hour regular meeting cadence.

Figure 2.2   Prototypical integration chain.

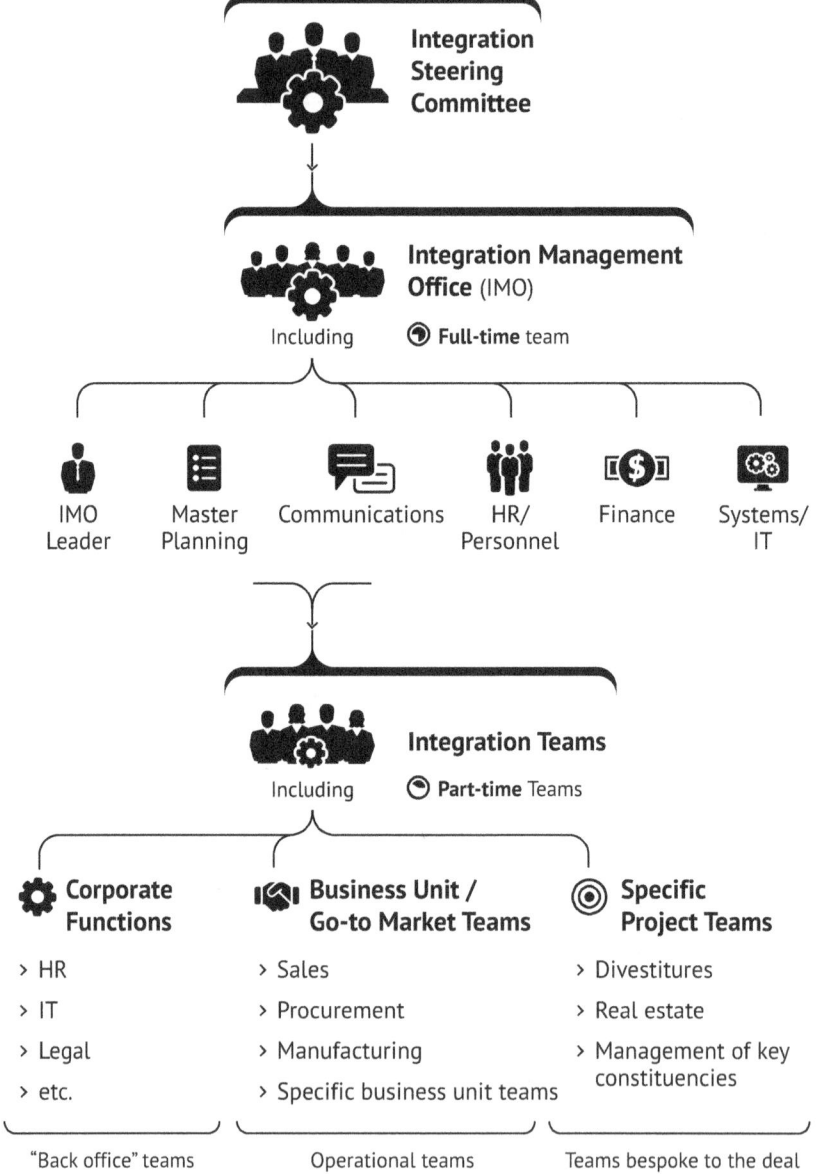

This decision did facilitate his team's input into the planning process—just not in a generative way. Over time, the senior leaders became increasingly fixated on aspects impacting their own direct field of vision, which bogged the process down considerably: with so many voices now needing to be heard, including from executives whose responsibilities had limited connection to the deal's goals, the planning team's bloated input diluted the focus of the effort. This invariably harmed more than the pace of the integration, as the core business oversight also became compromised. As a result, the CEO was forced to relaunch the process, costing the organization significant time, effort, momentum, and value.

This relatively banal case speaks to the criticality of the Parallel Process. This wasn't an effort plagued with drama or bad blood. The CEO simply ran things as he normally would, which, under normal circumstances, tended to work out fine. But a normal, "business as usual" way of operating doesn't align with the specific demands of the integration. The separation that the Parallel Process enforces allows integration planning to progress in a focused, timely, and effective manner, and it pre-empts the natural creep and delays that occur when too many voices advocate for special interests.

THE RESPONSIBILITIES AND CHALLENGES OF THE INTEGRATION CHAIN

Let's focus on the specific groups that make up the integration staffs. Each of these groups has a distinct set of responsibilities that contribute to the success of any integration. Figure 2.3 provides a general outline that the remainder of this section expands on.

Figure 2.3   Groups and responsibilities in the integration chain.

Integration Teams	IMO	Steering Committee
• Functional-level policies, processes, and resource allocations • Line manager leadership recommendations • Socialization of team decisions with business unit leaders	• Composition and sequence of Integration Teams • Integration deliverables (content and timing) • Integration milestones • Resolution of interdependencies • Triage of issues for escalation • Validation of value creation projects	• End-state organizational structure • Senior leadership appointments • Metrics of success • Value capture targets • Allocation of integration budget • Speed of integration • Approval of integration capital projects • Ratification of integration decisions

The Steering Committee (Steerco)

Sitting atop the integration hierarchy, Steerco's mandate is to ensure the combined organization realizes the goals set forth in the deal rationale. Its membership typically includes the original architects of the deal, like the CEOs of the acquiring and acquired companies, as well as the CFO of the acquirer, some kind of operational leader from the acquisition, and perhaps an additional member or two relating to the specific nature of the deal.

As a result, Steerco not only establishes the direction and fundamental parameters for the integration (including guiding principles for culture, as covered in Chapter Eight), but also selects those who'll oversee the project management (the IMO), resolves any questions when they reach an impasse, and gets final signoff on all major decisions. As Alexandra Lajoux aptly puts it, they're the ones asking and answering for the future combined organization, "*What* will we do and *who* will do it?"[1] Given their part-time commitment to the integration, as well as their oversight and appellate review responsibilities, a meeting every three weeks is typically sufficient for the Steerco to fulfill its role.

Steerco members (especially the acquiring CEO) often come equipped with decisions to enforce right off the bat as part of the direction-setting for the deal. For Doug Parker, who eyed American Airlines for its superior size and scale, he knew the integration needed to be operations-forward. He certainly had his non-negotiables, like keeping his senior management team (who he affectionately referred to as his "Band of Brothers"). At the same time, he knew US Airways had to do whatever it took to maintain American Airlines' strengths. That meant moving his team from Arizona to American Airlines' Dallas headquarters. He also ensured that the IMO was aligned around the deal's strategic rationale, entrusting it to them and their analyses to figure out how best to implement the integration.

The Integration Management Office

One level below the Steering Committee is the IMO. Extremely competent and hand-picked by Steerco, they orchestrate the integration such that the combined organization can accomplish the strategic directives of the deal, while also acting as the central repository for all the integration activity and data. Put simply, they are the control room for the entire integration effort. From setting strict timetables, deliverables, and reporting formats, to managing Steerco's agenda, determining what decisions need review, and even controlling the quality of the integration work (e.g., how much can we achieve in savings, what are the unintended costs), the IMO is the key project manager that makes sense of the integration chaos and drives every initiative forward. It's also often the only team drawn up and staffed full-time for the integration efforts.

The IMO's role changes over two broad phases of the integration effort. First, during the period post-deal announcement and pre-Day One, their responsibilities encompass intensive operational and organizational planning. Then, in the period post-Day One, their responsibilities transition to rigorous coordination. Though the specific balance will vary depending on the deal (a small acquisition or "business as usual" deal, e.g., often utilizes the IMO more as a coordinator), an IMO generally:[2]

- Drives the development of the integration masterplan (which subsumes plans for individual integration projects, communications, and synergy capture).
- Creates and oversees all integration processes (e.g., reporting and status updates, interdependency and issue resolution, cross-functional collaboration, etc.).
- Manages communications to stakeholders.
- Sets and maintains the pace of integration from planning through execution.
- Spearheads measurements and tracking across all Integration Teams, implements improvement methods if necessary, and selectively solicits and incorporates feedback.

It's no coincidence that these responsibilities comprise the focus of many of the remaining chapters, because while Steerco lays the groundwork and gets the final say, it's the IMO that drives the work of the integration. If you're interested in a more granular breakdown, Janice Roehl-Anderson has dedicated an entire chapter to the role of the IMO, which offers perspectives and materials of use beyond the book's nominal focus on IT in M&A, including sample templates and deliverables related to the office's work.[3]

The Integration Teams

Lastly, there are the Integration Teams who implement the integration efforts at the level of specific functional areas. Guided by the cadence and review process set by the IMO, these indispensable integration staffs develop the individual plans meant to realize synergy targets (concerning, e.g., cost, revenue, and assets). The IMO tasks each team with developing a plan to achieve desired synergies for a specific area: in the American Airlines deal, we started with as many as 29 teams, covering issues from fleet management and disaster recovery to airline associations and customer rewards (though that number was eventually combined and reduced). An Integration Leader—or sometimes multiple Integration Coleaders, as I'll cover in Chapter Three—is chosen according to their competence and relevance to the integration priority assigned to their respective team.

The members of the Integration Teams occupy an in-between position whose unique challenges both they themselves and the IMO should try to anticipate. Beyond the part-time split and related reporting complications, the Integration Team members are both "agents and recipients of change," meaning that they're contributing to the evolution of the organization just as they're simultaneously working through the ongoing disruptions of the integration, making sense of the ensuant change (e.g., culturally, environmentally), and likely even wondering what it will all mean for them on the other side.[4] The IMO can also exacerbate the discomforting ambiguity the Integration Teams face if they fail to provide sufficiently clear instructions, which (albeit unintentionally) forces the teams to make sense of management's vision themselves.[5]

The IMO can help combat this ambiguity through dedicated programming during the integration planning phase. A group from McKinsey, reflecting on successful engagements, has advocated for an "IMO-led boot camp" held over several days, during which the IMO "explained the deal rationale; set expectations for the path ahead, including responsibilities of all Integration Teams and leaders; and got the teams started on planning the integration effort."[6] Together with workshops that targeted key capabilities, like tracking progress toward synergy capture and addressing different work styles, this in-person programming helped align the Integration Teams concretely around the goals for the deal while simultaneously developing the competencies they would need to employ over the coming months.

SETTING UP FOR SUCCESS: COMPOSING THE IMO

The success of your integration depends on staffing your IMO with the right people in the right positions—a process that resonates with the construction of a professional basketball roster. In the very broadest of terms, General Managers tend to pursue two routes: a super team or a system team. Super teams are built around a group of all-star caliber players, each of whom is an elite individual contributor (think the early 2010s "Heatles" era Miami Heat built around LeBron James, Dwyane Wade, and Chris Bosh). A good system team, meanwhile, often features a few big-name players, but its success is built more around a coaching philosophy or way of playing that effectively leverages stars and role players alike to make the whole greater than the sum of the parts (think the 2023 Boston Celtics or the 2022 Denver Nuggets).

The ideal IMO combines the best of both approaches. Each member needs to be a superstar (or rising star), but the team must also have the structural support to empower them to execute their duties at the level required. Achieving this requires Steerco to understand what to look for in an IMO candidate, what positions the IMO will need (depending on the deal), the challenges they may face in recruiting for them (and how to overcome those challenges), as well as the actions they need to take to ensure that the IMO is fully empowered to realize its mandate. Let's start with the IMO Leader, who will serve as the lynchpin for the effort.

The IMO Leader: Signaling and Skills

The choice of IMO Leader carries an immense signaling power that Steerco should understand and utilize. The CFO, for example, might be an excellent candidate, but her selection may lead people to interpret the integration as a financially driven event, even if it's supposed to be operations-forward. What's more, it can also communicate what I call "seriousness of purpose" (or lack thereof). During the chaotic HP–Compaq merger, the two sides decided they would each nominate a coleader for the IMO (a decision I'll cover in Chapter Three). While Compaq chose CFO Jeff Clarke, an ascending star who would eventually become CEO of Kodak, HP went with a senior sales executive who had earned a great amount of respect over his long tenure with the company but was nearing retirement. These choices signaled a difference in importance and commitment to the IMO, one which raised questions about where power and influence would emanate from, despite HP being the acquirer.

Beyond what the choice might signal, there's also the fundamental question of skillset. As the person most responsible for ensuring that the integration is carried out according to plan, the IMO Leader must be able to serve as the pragmatic complement to Steerco's strategic prowess and are best when they can apply their depth of executional experience, their encyclopedic knowledge of the business, and their ability to stay cool under pressure. Whichever pool you choose to draw from, look for someone who embodies as many of the following qualities as possible:

- **Outstanding attention to detail.** Even the smallest error can cost the IMO—and thus the entire integration effort—precious time and energy. While mistakes happen, it's critical to manifest an atmosphere of diligence and care from the top down with a leader who lives and breathes accountability and teamwork in every interaction.
- **Superb team and talent management skills.** The IMO Leader is the individual lynchpin of the integration chain of command. They must be able to not only manage the IMO with the utmost competence, but also effectively leverage the many part-time integration staffs simultaneously juggling their base business responsibilities.
- **Empathy.** For all the spreadsheets and data that integration entails, we can't lose sight of the toll that it exacts from people throughout

the organization (some more than others). A candidate with great emotional intelligence, a light touch, and real empathy can often help anticipate how decisions will affect different groups of people (and proactively develop the appropriate measures), as well as respond appropriately when issues do arise. It's critical for this person to embody the mentality that "leaders eat last."

- **Cultural adaptability and rapport-building.** Culture is often a huge deal killer, something I'll cover more in Chapter Eight. The first cultural hurdle concerns coming together with those from the other side: you need an expert bridge-builder, someone who deeply appreciates and understands culture, respects diversity, and has a track record of bringing people together.

- **Strong cultural assessment and mapping skills.** The other cultural hurdle is structural, rather than interpersonal. An effective IMO Leader should not only respect *that* the other side has its own culture and way of doing things when planning for integration, but also be prepared to realistically assess which cultural elements from each side best suit the goals for the deal.

- **The ability to develop focused and effective internal and external communications plans.** The announcement is only the beginning. As I cover in Chapter Five, communications must anticipate and address the concerns, interests, and needs of stakeholders both internal and external on a cadence built around key milestones. While many IMOs will have someone else directly overseeing communications, the head of the team is no less vital in developing the messaging and guiding framework.

- **Friction mitigation skills.** In integration, the unexpected will invariably happen. Productively dealing with the unexpected—and the frictions it can create—constitutes an essential ad hoc skill that an IMO Leader should have in their toolkit.

Filling Out the IMO

Determining the remainder of the IMO roles follows a slightly different set of criteria. Oftentimes, the best candidates are two or three levels below the C-suite: young, aggressive, and high-potentials (if not the highest) in their respective functions, who also demonstrate the ability to think beyond their functions. As my former McKinsey colleague James McLetchie wrote, the IMO "should be conceived as a vehicle to test and reveal the 'leadership of tomorrow.'"[7] As a shorthand, here's how I've condensed my thinking to countless curious CEOs: "If you don't get a lot of yelling and screaming from their bosses when you propose putting them on the team, then they're the wrong people."

This comes down to two reasons. First, the role is extremely challenging, making it best suited for someone slightly more junior who's hungry for more learning, more doing, and more impact. But even more fundamentally, since you have to divvy up your resources to steer the integration and maintain the base business simultaneously, it makes sense to keep the function heads where they are to maintain top-line growth. In practice, this might mean appointing your deputy comptroller rather than your head of finance: in so doing, you keep a steady hand guiding business as usual through a period of volatility while still bolstering the integration effort with significant financial acumen and knowledge of the organization.

IMO Roles

Unlike so many integration elements that vary by deal, the size of the IMO runs fairly consistent. Across all the deals I've supported, a small group has always sufficed: five to eight people in most cases. Even for massive projects—say, a merger between two huge steel companies (albeit with a very centralized organization and a command-and-control CEO)—a six-person team was all that was needed. Because the IMO's work represents a significant strategic and project management undertaking, it needs to be lean to allow its members to work together seamlessly, efficiently, and at pace.

There are also specific roles that most, if not all, IMOs should have, which divide roughly into two types. Though overlap of course occurs, some roles are focused more on process, while others address an area of specific relevance to the deal. While the specific makeup of your IMO should reflect the priorities stemming from the deal rationale, the list below covers the kinds of positions that most often contribute to smooth integration:

- **IMO Leader.** The direct link to the Steering Committee, the IMO Leader commands the organization of integration efforts to accomplish the goals for the deal, translating the rationale into actionable principles and guidelines with key deliverables and criteria. To synthesize the section above, this role requires someone of the highest competence, someone you can trust to work with closely on matters of serious consequence.

- **Deputy to the Integration Leader.** This is the chief-of-staff position for the IMO, both the backbone of the team and the oil that keeps the cogs moving. The deputy's role is immensely administrative, encompassing ensuring project teams are launched, tracking their progress, and putting together agendas for IMO meetings. I can't overstate how numerous the administrative and logistical tasks are during integration—and it falls on the deputy to make sure everything gets done.

- **Master Planning.** Another intense administrative role, this person takes point in creating the masterplan for the entire integration. This person ensures that every process and individual plan fits together concretely and comprehensively, working closely with the Integration Teams to ensure their plans can stand alone and interdependently. They are vital to the planning covered in Chapter Four.

- **Finance.** Unsurprisingly, given the overarching objective of the integration to create value, the IMO will need someone who can determine if the business is on track to create financial synergies. This person is in the best position to assess whether there's sufficient capital to do all that's necessary to achieve the integration goals over a (roughly) three-year period. Think of this person as the CFO for the integration, the bookkeeper overseeing baselining, value creation, tracking the revenue synergies to be counted, and other financial elements addressed in Chapter Four.

- **HR/Personnel.** This individual understands the talent that exists in the organization. But being knowledgeable is a given. This person must also be savvy about how HR works and what resources are available. As the go-to for personnel and staffing, they will spearhead the Personnel Cascade, the sequential leadership selection process covered in Chapter Six. They'll likely also be the ones to oversee the consultants brought in to support the integration. For example, if a consultant is hired to help integrate the two compensation packages for the merged entities, it should likely fall to the HR member to orchestrate their work.

- **Communications.** This person has the unenviable job of overseeing all the internal and external communications during the integration—a role that is as significant as it is intense. Managing all these voices, let alone the multitude of internal streams that make up the torrent that is integration, takes a resolve of steel. This was true even years ago: when I supported US Airways and American Airlines, for example, I recall a Dallas newspaper running a weekly column that charted the integration's developments. Today, the challenge is even greater, as they will need to provide information about the team's program to the CEO, board, and other internal stakeholders, as well as traditional media, in addition to handling the social media storm. This means you need someone you can trust to put out information perfectly clearly—in a way that is hard to misconstrue—as well as monitor and report back on what others are saying about the company's integration efforts.

- **Systems.** IT often sets the pace for integration. Managing one system can be a headache under normal circumstances; combining two companies can be problematic. Since your ability to move forward will depend on how quickly the team can build a unified system to support their objectives, you'll need an expert who can find common technological ground—which is much easier said than done.

You might need other roles depending on your deal. Merck and Schering-Plough, for example, needed someone with deep research and development expertise, as well as someone who could help manage a spinoff. While there is no single definitive list that you can follow, every IMO member must advance the team toward increased alignment with the deal's motivating purpose.

Recruiting Challenges

Even if you've identified the perfect cast for each IMO role, recruiting them isn't always easy. You want these folks because they're the best of the best—which is just the reason why their team will fight to keep them. But in the end, you can't take no for an answer: successful integration is now the prime objective of your organization, and it must be all hands on deck to accomplish it.

I liken it to a lesson my father once taught me. Over the course of his long career of service to the United States, Eugene Fubini became adept at identifying talent and working the system to ensure they ended up in the right place to advance the mission. He had started at the Pentagon after emigrating from Italy across troubled waters and dedicating himself to the American cause. By the early 1960s, he had been selected to serve as the

Assistant Secretary of Defense under President Kennedy. With tensions flaring as the Cold War threatened to turn hot, the United States spared no resource in combating threats both foreign and domestic, and my father found himself in an environment where every branch and department, though united under the same flag, competed fiercely to address what each considered the top priority. It was from this crucible that he emerged to serve the Defense Science Board, now the longest-serving advisory board providing science and technology solutions to the Department of Defense (DoD).

Fast forward to the Clinton administration, and as the head of the Defense Science Board, my father came to know a certain Air Force colonel. His decades of experience told him that this colonel would be a tremendous asset to the appointed Secretary of Defense, so he advised the Secretary: instruct the Air Force to put him on a plane first thing Monday morning, ready to support the DoD on a new assignment. But when my father checked back in, he was surprised to learn that, despite the request, the Air Force had refused. The colonel played a critical role in a priority program, the response had been, and the Secretary was wary of upsetting an important Air Force commander. Donning the cap of the stern advisor that came to define his proud career of service, my father responded: "No, you don't understand. You're in charge. You're not *asking* for him. You're insisting that you need him."

You can't settle for second or third best with integration. While it might create discomfort (that's integration in a nutshell), insist on getting the right person for the IMO, no matter who that person is, and make it clear that for the next four or five months, it's the IMO that receives top priority. Otherwise, what might seem like a polite concession could hamper the team and risk compromising the entire effort altogether.

Sometimes the reluctance stems from the candidates themselves. Most often, they're afraid that taking time away from their "main job" for a temporary support role will hamper their career in some way. Over the last few years, there seems to be growing recognition of the positive impacts integration service can have on a career,[8] but all the same, it's best to come equipped with compelling arguments when making the ask:

1. **They will learn more about integration in their months on the team than they can learn anywhere else.** IMO work is an unparalleled opportunity to learn how to bring together disparate parts of the business into a well-functioning whole, a skill that will be increasingly valuable not only for future acquisitions, but for any restructuring effort.

2. **For three to five months, they'll be among the most powerful people in the company.** The future of the organization is in their hands, and their decisions will shape the business for years to come. As part of their IMO responsibilities, they'll work closely with business unit heads, the CEO, and even board members. The connections they make during their IMO tenure will serve their careers well. This is a truly rare, if not once in a lifetime, opportunity.

3. **It's uniquely hard work for a uniquely qualified leader.** You will of course need to be honest with team candidates about the reality of the role. As I've often said, "It's a great job. The bad news is that you'll never want to do it again." The fact of the matter is that it's an enormous amount of work under intense deadlines. They must understand that they're going to have to work hard—likely harder than they've ever had to before. They'll have to have difficult conversations and tell senior people no, as well as deal with an ocean of "what if" scenarios that require Olympic-level mental gymnastics. But they're the one being asked because they're the right person for this tough job. This is the time for them to step up and show everyone what they're made of.

Empowering the IMO

This chapter has covered a lot of important ground, but I want to place added emphasis on this: the IMO *must* be given the authority to get things done. They must be fully empowered. Establishing the dual chains of command is the first step, but committing to the Parallel Process—meaningfully empowering the IMO—often requires persistent resolve and intentionality. Before I get into the mechanics of how and why, allow me to set the scene.

You're the CEO of a company that has just recently closed a major deal with a regional competitor. In the early stages of integration planning, your head of HR comes to you with a proposal: "We've been talking for months about launching the Future Leaders Program. What if we factored that into the cultural integration, so we can start developing the best and brightest from both sides into the right kind of leaders for the merged org?" Given contextual factors, you recognize that the proposal makes some sense.

You have a decision to make at this juncture. She's one of your trusted leaders, and it's vital that you give her the ability to lead her unit, so under normal circumstances, you might give her the green light to at least evaluate the plan's feasibility in more detail. But granting her request, even if the plan ends up being a good one, runs counter to the Parallel Process you must maintain. Now you've opened the floodgates for other business unit leaders to pitch their ideas—with the tacit acknowledgment that they can simply sidestep the IMO if a disagreement arises.

All integration decisions must run through the IMO, though there are power dynamics that can make this a trying adjustment. For senior functional leaders, instead of interfacing directly with the chief executive as they're used to, they're now expected to go through a team whose members are *otherwise their juniors*—and who might say no! The flipside of this coin puts the IMO members into an uncomfortable position: they'll likely need to tell the people who are otherwise their superiors that they can't provide them with the talent, money, or other resources if they feel their superiors' requests lack alignment with the objectives for the integration. Steerco (especially the CEO anointed to run the merged company) must firmly and consistently reinforce the dual command structure to allow the Parallel Process to work to maximum effect, particularly early in the planning stage.

Empowering the IMO also means selectively limiting their availability to field unsolicited input. This is yet another difficult balance to strike. Holed up in its own office away from the rest of the organization, the IMO doesn't want to come across as hostile or cold—in fact, it'll need to gather perspectives from across the organization as part of its efforts to plan, tailor, and implement the integration. At the same time, in dispelling any such perceptions, it also can't risk becoming the "complaint department."[9] To avoid an incessant stream of disgruntled voices and pet projects pitched as integration opportunities, Steerco should support the IMO in maintaining a tight schedule where only a few, regularly occurring slots are designated as "doors open." Beyond those windows, the IMO should control not only when it solicits feedback, but also on what and from whom, according to its emergent needs. It cannot risk getting bogged down to the detriment of its main priorities.

INTEGRATION ROLES AND THE ARCHITECTURE TO SUPPORT THEM

In reality, the personnel choices covered in this chapter aren't made in a vacuum. It's one thing to have the right people in the right places, but it's another to have the right architecture in place to guide their work in the right direction. While the fundamental base is the Parallel Process, in the next chapter, I'll explore some of the major architectural design points that Steerco will need to decide on at the outset of integration planning. Similarly shaped by the deal rationale, these decisions will start to fill in some of the questions that this chapter tabled, like whether to appoint one or two leaders to head an Integration Team, and will shine more light on how to equip the integration side of the dual command chain to accomplish Steerco's vision for the deal.

ACTION ITEMS IN REVIEW

- **Enforce the Parallel Process**—separate management of "business as usual" from integration activities to preserve base business momentum and streamline integration decision-making.
- **Staff the IMO with the most promising high-potentials in the areas that the needs of the integration demand**—and don't take no for an answer.
- **Fully empower the IMO**—ensure all integration decisions go through them (prevent end runs around them) and support them in minimizing unsolicited feedback.
- **Ensure alignment between the IMO and Integration Teams**—support the IMO in hosting in-person programming that clarifies the goals and reasons for the deal and targets integration-related skill building.

CHAPTER THREE

ALIGNING YOUR VISION: THE INTEGRATION ARCHITECTURE

W e're fond of analogies for leadership at the Harvard Business School. In the Organizational Behavior Unit, we often teach of the leader as beacon (vision), as coach (motivation), as innovator (new growth opportunities), as change agent (adaptation).[1] An effective leader must develop and demonstrate each of these facets, we instruct our students, whether they're MBAs or executives. M&A and integration leadership is no exception—in fact, it's a realm that pushes leaders to embody these facets the most.

There's one facet that becomes particularly prominent: the leader as architect. In the big picture, as my fellow faculty have explained, this aspect is all about setting the building blocks for organizational success: "Part of a leader's job is to equip the organization to transform inputs into outputs by defining organizational strategy, shaping organizational identity, and then managing four organizational components—formal organizational structure, culture, people, and critical tasks—such that each component, and their interaction, aligns to produce performance."[2] Leadership, in this sense, requires aligning the "hard" and "soft" components of the organization in light of macro conditions and mitigating factors to render the outputs that determine success. But this isn't the whole picture for integration. In addition to creating alignment within the merging organization through the integration effort, leaders must also first align the integration effort itself around their vision for the new organization.

This chapter introduces the critical decisions that will inform the effort's alignment—what I call the *integration architecture*. Framed as a series of bounded choices, these decisions will help determine the approach and guiding principles of your effort from the outset of the planning process. Throughout the discussion, Doug Parker and the US Airways–American Airlines integration will act as a lens into the tradeoffs that each option presents. After surveying these options, we'll also get into the kinds of factors that decision-makers should consider, supplemental to the deal rationale, in determining the right architectural approach for their integration.

MAJOR ARCHITECTURAL DESIGN POINTS

There are four major points of integration architecture that top integration management should decide on prior to or at the very start of integration planning. This isn't an exhaustive list—culture, for example, will take up the entirety of Chapter Eight. Nor are there any universal right or wrong decisions. Rather than approaching these decisions normatively, we'll consider how Parker and his team evaluated the tradeoffs as they prepared for their complex integration between two former rival airlines.[3]

IMO Leadership: Sole or Coleader?

Integration architecture starts with the IMO: will it have a single leader or two coleaders? Since this choice shapes the effectiveness of the IMO itself (which must function extremely effectively), there are, of course, interpersonal factors to consider. But as a matter of integration design, this choice signals the balance and tone of the integration effort, and by the same token, the merged entity that's taking shape. In short, the guiding question becomes: "Is this a merger, or a takeover?" Putting aside the nuances and exceptions, going with a single IMO Leader typically falls in the "takeover" camp, while opting for a shared leadership model clearly communicates a more collaborative "merger" (see Figure 3.1).

But reality is often more complicated than the binary of "total takeover" versus "true merger of equals." There are plenty of deals that are purposefully construed as mergers to try to generate collective buy-in and goodwill, though one side is really more in control than the other. This isn't to say that the title of "merger" is disingenuous in these cases: while one side might have specific elements that they'll adamantly implement, their vision for the combined organization makes the potential upsides of a merger approach more attractive, despite the unique challenges. But even so, does it make

Figure 3.1 IMO leadership: sole or coleader?

Sole IMO Leader	IMO Coleader
• Signals takeover	• Signals collaborative merger
• Streamlines decision-making	• Could facilitate buy-in from both sides
• Could hinder (esp. acquired) buy-in	• Politics and differences of opinion could create tension and slow down process

sense to go with a co-led IMO to signal a merger if it also risks complicating how easily the relative acquirer can implement its vision?

Doug Parker wrangled with this question as he began planning for the integration with American Airlines. He had no trouble deciding on the leader from the US Airways side: Robert Isom. His exceptionally skilled COO and seeming heir apparent, Isom had prior integration experience and a track record that aligned perfectly with the goals of such an operations-forward effort. But this deal insisted upon a shared IMO. The two sides had clearly different philosophies, and there was no hiding the contentious atmosphere that had developed over the course of the negotiations. Even as Parker adopted the American Airlines moniker and agreed to maintain the "acquired" headquarters, the legacy US Airways team was mindful of dispelling the air of hostility.

Parker thus looked to Beverly Goulet. The former Treasurer during American Airlines' bankruptcy process, she had emerged as a clear leader during the negotiations with US Airways, one who both sides came to respect as fair and balanced, and critically someone who Parker felt was bought into his team's vision for the new organization. Even so, behind the scenes, Isom was made first among equals and given more authority over time. The IMO thus had two coleaders, signaling (and making good on) the deal's goals as a merger, though the balance of their joint leadership tipped slightly more toward legacy US Airways, as did the reality of the effort overall.

This dynamic was essentially flipped for the HP–Compaq integration. In Chapter Two, I mentioned that HP's representative—a senior sales executive who was respected but nearing retirement—didn't stack up well against Compaq's champion in Jeff Clarke. The mismatch in perceived "seriousness of purpose" put HP at a disadvantage in planning and implementing the integration for which it was nominally the acquirer. Clarke was not only perceived as the stronger force, but he also exerted stronger influence over the integration effort than he might have with a better-matched counterpart. This case has since served as a valuable lesson: the balance of power among IMO Coleaders can meaningfully influence the future of the emerging company, which further underscores the kind of person most suited for this work.

Integration Team Leadership: "One in a Box" or "Two in a Box"?

Once Steerco settles the IMO leadership, it's time for the chosen IMO Leader(s) to make a similar set of decisions: should the Integration Teams be staffed with a single leader ("one in a box") or two coleaders ("two in a box")? As with the IMO leadership decision, these choices send different signals and have different implications for integration planning (see Figure 3.2). "Two in a box" staffs an Integration Team with a coleader from either side: this sends a message of parity and collaboration, though the debates it produces within teams can devolve from productive to dysfunctional as pressures mount (including, notably, which of the two will keep their job in the new organization). "One in a box," meanwhile, often features a leader from the acquiring side and prioritizes efficiency of process and decision-making over signaling parity (though I've seen staff leave in

Figure 3.2   Integration Team leadership: "one in a box" or "two in a box"?

One in a Box	Two in a Box
• Signals enforcement	• Signals parity and collaboration
• Streamlines decision-making	• Could contribute best of both sides
• Could hinder buy-in	• Could create tension and slow down process

droves once it's clear their side is the "loser," which threatened to derail the integration altogether).

The deal rationale can help weigh the relative tradeoffs in making these decisions. To begin with, the teams don't need to follow the same structure down the line: where the buyer wants to strictly maintain their way of doing things, for example, "one in a box" likely makes more sense, while areas that require a more delicate balance between the two sides might benefit from "two in a box." Even among co-led teams, the balance between the leaders can vary. An integration between two Nordic multinationals (where the buyer was clearly perceived as the lead) featured several teams led by someone from the acquired firm (bolstered by a supporting "co-lead" from the acquirer).[4] The US Airways–American Airlines integration also had "two in a box" teams where the coleader from the American Airlines side played an especially vital role given Steerco's decision to maintain certain legacy American Airlines systems (which I'll get into below). And when co-led teams reached an impasse, the IMO stepped in to resolve things, even escalating to Steerco if needed, and used the deal rationale to determine whose way better fit the integration's needs.

Systems and Timing: "Adopt and Go" or "Best of Both"?

This decision boils down to one of integration's most fundamental tradeoffs: do we prioritize speed, or do we take the time up front to optimize system performance for the long term? For the "adopt and go" approach, planners identify the best of the existing legacy systems and adopt them essentially wholesale. This is all about speed and up-front efficiency in advancing the integration with as few disruptions as possible: while neither company's booking system might be totally ideal, Company A's is the better of the two, so you go with that and put off upgrading it until after the integration is complete. "Best of both," meanwhile, means taking a close look at

Figure 3.3   Systems: "adopt and go" or "best of both"?

Adopt and Go	Best of Both
• Speed* • Adopting legacy systems wholesale*	• Long-term effectiveness • Investigating, redesigning/weaving together programs with the long term in mind

both companies' systems and, after analyzing their respective strengths and weaknesses, devising a way to weave both operations together to create superior performance and results. This approach is far more time- and labor-intensive up front, so the tradeoff is slowing down the integration in the hopes of increased long-term optimization (see Figure 3.3).

Parker favored the "adopt and go" approach for the US Airways–American Airlines integration, though it was not without tradeoffs. His prior integration experience and familiarity with other airline mergers—not known for their ease of execution—convinced him that optimizing for speed would better contribute to deal success: ideally, it would score quick wins that built momentum early and would make it easier for the base business to continue through the integration's disruptions. Since legacy American Airlines was the larger of the two airlines, often its systems were adopted for the "new American Airlines," although many of them were already out of date. At the same time, it wasn't lost on the legacy American Airlines side just how much of "their way" was being chosen for the new organization, which calcified into pockets of resistance against Parker's cultural vision.

Sub-option: "Integrate Now, Innovate Later" or "Redesign for the Future?"

Going with the "adopt and go" approach unlocks a further set of systems decisions: Which of the systems you've adopted will you need to update, and when? "Integrate now, innovate later" maintains the essential speed of

Figure 3.4   Systems (continued): "integrate now, innovate later" or "redesign for the future"?

*If Adopt and Go	
Integrate Now, Innovate Later	**Redesign for the Future**
• Speed • Commit to launching the organization as quickly as possible by adopting legacy systems as-is	• Long-term effectiveness • Use integration as time to upgrade selected legacy systems and implement further change

"adopt and go" by committing to a system, regardless of its state, all the way through the integration effort to eliminate as many short-term stoppages as possible, even if a system is already or soon to be out of date at the start of integration. "Redesign for the future," on the other hand, means allocating the time and capital up front to upgrade the adopted system at the risk of slowing down and drawing out integration. The tradeoffs are thus quite similar to the decision above, with the key difference between "best of both" and "redesign for the future" coming down to whether you create something new from both companies, or you improve off the base that one company already has established (see Figure 3.4).

Parker hated the thought of "not innovating," but speed remained his top priority. As a result, his IMO embraced "integrate now" as much as possible under the "adopt and go" umbrella, postponing most upgrades until after the integration when the combined management team could evaluate the needs of the new organization more clearly. Some exceptions had to be made as the IMO and Integration Teams uncovered more data: the planners had anticipated adopting the legacy American Airlines HR system wholesale and importing the US Airways data, for example, but emergent concerns around the system's ability to scale with the expanding company forced them to pivot in real time.

In cases like this, the organization had to continue running their own systems in parallel while groups from HR and IT worked to develop a new solution.

BASIC FACTORS TO CONSIDER WHEN DETERMINING INTEGRATION ARCHITECTURE

The deal rationale remains the fundamental determinant for these architectural designs, but there are plenty of interrelated factors that can bring added clarity to the decision-making process. Here are the things that, at a minimum, leaders should consider in determining the architecture for their integration:

- Strategic rationale for the acquisition
- Business case for the purchase price
- Key deal stakeholders
- Short-term goals
- Long-term vision
- Initial sources of value
- Deal assumptions and risks
- Acquired entity's organizational structure, capabilities, and technologies
- Acquired entity's financial structure (revenue streams and cost structure)
- Acquired entity's operating model
- Areas of overlap with existing business
- Unique transition requirements

In sum, there is no "right" or "wrong" way in setting up integration architecture; only ways that are more or less aligned with the many factors motivating the deal.

ACTION ITEMS IN REVIEW

- **Use the deal rationale and other fundamental motivators to determine the appropriate integration design for your deal's goals.** This includes the representation of each company among integration leadership and how to handle systems integration.
- **Allow room for case-by-case exceptions to general guiding architectural principles in areas of exceptional need.** Even with a largely "two in a box" approach, some teams may be better suited with a single leader, or under an "adopt and go" and "integrate now" paradigm of speed, you may find you need to selectively update certain systems as part of the immediate integration effort. The overarching goal is not to be prescriptive, but to determine the balance that best accommodates each of your deal's needs.

PART II

PLAN: PREPARING THE INTEGRATION

CHAPTER FOUR

IF YOU MEASURE IT, CHANGE WILL COME: SETTING BASELINES, TRACKING PROGRESS, AND THE INTEGRATION MASTERPLAN

" **Y**ou don't know what you really bought until you look under the hood." Elise Eberwein, former Executive Vice President of People, Communications, and Public Affairs for US Airways, addressed a packed room, its semicircular rows evocative of a Roman theater. On this chilly Wednesday afternoon, a group of nearly 100 M&A specialists had gathered as part of Harvard's annual Mergers and Acquisitions executive education program to learn about the realities of integration directly from one of Doug Parker's most trusted leaders. A vital contributor to the success of the merger with American Airlines, Elise had been through it all.

"Did you meet all your targets?" one of the executives asked. They met many of them, she told us, but it took longer than expected to get there. American Airlines' bankruptcy may have catalyzed the US Airways bid, but it also meant that the airline had been underinvesting in key systems for years. They achieved many of their synergy goals two years into the integration, but it wasn't until the Covid-19 pandemic was winding down nearly eight years in (or, perhaps, precisely *because* of the mutual enemy it represented) that they finally had a culturally united company. But the lesson from those early days was clear: due diligence could only account for so much.

To extend Elise's metaphor, the merger's leadership represented a very talented group of "drivers," but no matter how clear the vision, how sound the strategic planning, how thorough the due diligence, or even how much ability there was "behind the wheel," the specifics of the integration depended on what they found "under the hood." This threw a few wrenches into Doug Parker's "adopt and go" approach, as the systems they had no choice but to adopt were sometimes painfully out of date. If Doug and his team wanted to achieve their goals for the merger, the integration had to account for the reality they found only once the airlines came together. It required a carefully designed, thoroughly detailed integration masterplan.

This chapter makes the case for thorough integration planning through the lens of the masterplan and a fundamental truth from Chapter One: setting goals and measuring results. We'll first discuss why the insufficiency of due diligence requires you to get zealous about measuring across both sides of the combined organization. The remaining bulk of the chapter is then reserved for the "how" that gives shape to this measuring principle. After touching on identifying and evaluating synergy targets, including factoring in the hidden transformational synergies that can help "unfreeze" your organization during the integration frenzy, I home in on baselining, the foundational practice that allows you to measure the progress of your integration. I then tie all this together into the essential components of and best practices for an integration masterplan.

PRELUDE: DUE DILIGENCE— AND ITS LIMITATIONS

What's the point of due diligence? This might sound like a ridiculous thing to ask about something that's quite literally required for M&A success. Its necessity, however, has impacted how many organizations approach and rely on due diligence—in ways that are mutually destructive of deal value. On the one hand, I've seen far too many acquirers *underestimate* the importance of the process by treating it as a financial formality instead of committing to an extensive examination of the acquisition target. And on the other hand (sometimes, paradoxically, even in the same transaction), I've found leaders *overestimate* its value by assuming its findings will automatically translate to smooth integration.

Let's agree to some known "truths": due diligence is meant to responsibly inform your acquisition decision, accurately gauge anticipated values, and ensure fundamentals are in place to move forward. At a high level, it validates your deal rationale and clears the way to closing your deal at a proper valuation, or, borrowing from Sirower and Weirens, it "tests the investment thesis of the deal—its value creation logic and how that value will be captured."[1] It's also an exercise in risk management, as Deloitte's Center for Board Effectiveness asserts: "a robust due diligence process [should be] designed to ferret out potential risks and valuation considerations, assess their magnitude and the probability of the risks' occurrence, consider whether mitigation is possible, and respond accordingly."[2] To break that into constituent parts, as Lajoux does, its purpose is "to confirm the existence of assets ... to assess the quality of leadership and human capital ... to check for potential future legal problems ... [and] to ensure that the paperwork of the deal is in order..."[3]

The first problem is that most organizations do too little diligence beyond the financials. This is like choosing to take a photo with low resolution: the resultant image might trace the contours and colors of what you're trying to capture, but it leaves out the granular contrasts and nuance that would convey the subject's true complexity. Acquirers that settle only for financial diligence are often shocked by the degree of difference they find in their acquisition, much to the complication of their integration efforts.

The remedy, as I argued in the *Harvard Business Review*, is to conduct an "outside-in" organizational diligence that assesses the target's institutional strengths and redundancies, investigates its ways of working (culture), and analyzes its various stakeholders to consider external challenges that a purely internal look could miss.[4] In practice, this entails interviewing a cross-section of key leaders from both companies, as well as common suppliers, key customers, analysts, and even former members of the acquisition target in parallel with the standard financial negotiations. Altogether, this process aims to better answer the question: What are the likely challenges we will face as we integrate these two complex companies over the next one to two years?

But even with more comprehensive diligence, a second problem remains: due diligence is more speculative than reality, more confirmatory than exhaustive. Planning for integration—actually combining two organizations—requires an even further level of scrutiny and insight. Rather than confirming *that* the deal is viable, integration planning must get deep into the details of *how* the two companies will come together to produce the deal's expected value. Even with diligence that aims to anticipate the critical issues that will underpin integration and inform the timeline and costs associated with them,[5] your inquiry is capped by a fundamental pre-close information barrier.

Elise's comment about looking "under the hood" speaks exactly to this barrier. Again, extending the analogy, you can research widely on the make and model of the car that's right for you, you can scrupulously pick the dealer you find most trustworthy, and you even might be able to get the Carfax report on the specific vehicle you've set your sights on, but no matter how much information you gather on it, there's bound to be quirks that you can't account for until it's yours.

PREPARING THE PLAN: IT STARTS WITH MEASURING

As the ultimate test of change management, integration demands careful attention to performance tracking, just as much as it requires a clear articulation of target goals. While the end goals tend to consume the bulk of leaders' attention, any pragmatist will tell you that end goals mean nothing without knowing how close (or far) you are from achieving them. It's first through measuring that you're able to catalyze the change needed to reach your goals. The converse is also true: if you don't measure it, it won't change.

Measuring consists of three components (Figure 4.1). Of course, it requires you to clearly establish and define your target goals in line with your deal rationale (where you're going). Those target goals will then inform the metrics you'll need to regularly track throughout the integration (your progress). And in order to contextualize your progress and

Figure 4.1   The three components of measuring.

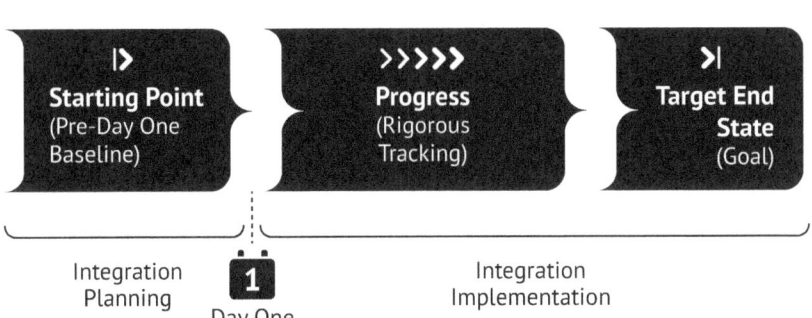

how much work there is to go, you must establish baselines for where you stand at the start of integration (where you've come from). It's only by committing to all three components that you can derive full value from measuring—en route to securing full potential value from your deal.

A Measuring Mindset: Why "Measuring" Over "Data"

I've noticed a significant change in response to this counsel over the years. These days, executives seem almost relieved. That's fantastic, they'll say, because we're such a data-driven company. By this, they mean that they have the *capacity* to measure. They have the tools and analytical chops to gather and make sense of data in ways that their counterparts 20 or 30 years ago could only dream of. But their premature relief underscores a fascinating irony: despite having better capacity to measure, many organizations today are less prepared to measure *well*.

The source of this irony lies in the distinction between data and measuring. Data has been and continues to be the word of our current moment. The data-driven decision-making paradigm that I alluded to in Chapter One, for example, is a quintessential example. But its ubiquity has also rendered it a deceptively nebulous term. It has become a good unto itself, particularly for decision-makers who aren't as close to the ground; one that tacitly values the quantity over the quality and relevance of what's gathered.

Measuring, meanwhile, demands specificity. It emphasizes process: it forces leaders to ask not only what data to collect, but also in what ways and how often. It remains close to the higher-order rationale, its repetition continually prompting leaders to evaluate why they're measuring what they're measuring, whether they're measuring the right things, and whether their anticipated target is still correct, as they make sense of the information they're taking in.

You must fight against the false presumption that data-gathering capacity will automatically translate to integration work—that it will just happen because "that's what we do." More often, the harsh reality is that integration's intense pace will push part-time Integration Team leaders to prioritize the unfamiliar (like connecting with their counterparts from the other side) and devote less attention to what might feel more familiar (tracking). But your entire integration chain of command must commit to the measuring process from the start in order to achieve target synergies. Otherwise, teams risk wasting limited time and resources on gathering irrelevant data, or even moving in the wrong direction, requiring costly course-correcting later in the game.

Measuring in Practice

Let me briefly address what kinds of things one measures in integration and the practical importance of doing so. Since Timothy Galpin and Mark Herndon dedicate an entire chapter of their book, *The Complete Guide to Mergers and Acquisitions*, to "merger measurement systems," I recommend looking there if you're interested in practicable resources like sample templates, process walkthroughs, and scorecards.[6] For our purposes, here are the four major measurement categories that they helpfully identify and the question that each is supposed to address:

- **Integration process measures.** "Is the integration progressing as planned to realize the goals for the deal?" (e.g., surveys of Integration Leaders and task force members)
- **Operational measures.** "Is the base business continuing [unaffected]?" (e.g., looking out for sudden shifts from normal behavior related to productivity, quality, and safety)
- **Cultural measures.** "Are the parts of the organization coming together in the intended direction?" (e.g., employee surveys, focus groups)
- **Financial measures.** "Are we meeting expected synergies?" (e.g., progress reports on efforts toward expected synergy capture)

Beyond the necessity for informing progress toward target objectives, measuring also supports integration efforts in the following ways:

- **Motivation.** A regular measuring cadence keeps Integration Teams motivated and on track to meet their target goals at the pace that's needed.
- **Accountability.** Measuring synergies versus a baseline ensures that individual Integration Teams remain grounded in their recommendations to the IMO and can't simply assert (or invent) changes to achieve savings or growth without basis.
- **Stakeholder confidence.** Measuring provides you with valuable data you can share with stakeholders, both external (analysts, shareholders) and internal (management, employees), to demonstrate what the deal has and continues to achieve.

The Challenge of Measuring and the Irony of Uncertainty

The commitment to measuring is much easier said (and argued) than done. Later in this chapter, I'll discuss what goes into an integration plan, but before we get there, we need to consider what measuring might actually look like in your integration. In particular, I want to highlight some of the complications that make this kind of measuring more challenging than expected. From procedural impediments that arise from integration's countless uncertainties to fundamental ambiguities around what leaders should actually be measuring, the complications can assume all sorts of forms. Let's consider an example.

Imagine you're the coleader of the HR Integration Team. You know with certainty that the combined organization won't need all of the product management staff from both sides past Day One (once both sides formally come together with the legal close). You also know that the new organizational structure will likely change the distributed nature of your organization's resources. Based on the merger model that's guiding the integration, you're looking first to obtain combinational synergies by eliminating duplicate staff. Also factoring in the added efficiencies that you anticipate from increasing shared services, as well as the forthcoming deployment of AI-enabled systems that were announced as part of the deal, you're looking at about a 25% reduction in staff. In order to achieve that reduction, you'll need to establish a baseline ("25% of what?"), as well as a way to measure the changes (cuts) being made across different groups of staff.

This proves more complicated than you anticipate. First, your company wasn't able to get specific headcounts prior to the deal close, so you'll need to coordinate with your coleader from the acquired company, despite palpable tensions. Second, it turns out that some of the acquired product teams came over in another deal a few years prior; faced with bigger-picture systems issues, they ended up keeping them on separate profit and loss statements in an unintegrated form. On top of that, many of the project managers are housed within a cross-functional department and play multiple roles, including scrum master and customer success, which raises questions about how they should be counted against headcount, and whether they're even reducible. And what's more, as a result of these edge cases, the files you're receiving from the acquired HR department don't always follow the same format as each other or your own.

In this scenario, you can't take for granted even forming a baseline measurement, let alone working toward achieving your synergy target. And even then, we're only talking about headcount. What if, as is so often the case, the target is much less clearly defined, like making your teams nimbler, more creative, or more diverse? Or, instead of team makeup, say the goal is to increase customer retention rates by 10%, but you don't have a clear grasp on the underlying mechanisms behind your company's retention problem, let alone the customer segments of the acquired company. When faced with so many unknowns, where do you begin?

There's an irony hidden in this challenge: the goal of measuring is to increase your precision and aim en route to your target, but the timing and hurdles of integration can make taking precise measurements exceedingly difficult. This irony is a characteristic case for the Uncertainty Principle, where leaders must get comfortable working from a 70 or 80% confidence level. Your IMO likely won't be able to take completely precise measurements, but even taking the effort to formulate specific metrics, gather as complete a picture of the relevant data as possible (in reasonable time), and track progress while refining the search parameters along the way will increase the efficacy of each team's efforts. And since most synergy targets are aspirational, meaning that the IMO inflates them to set expectations high and keep focus up, some lack of precision is acceptable—so long as you are consistently measuring.

BEST PRACTICES FOR SYNERGY PLANNING

I won't get into the technicalities behind synergy calculations and the mathematical regressions that can factor into appropriate deal valuation—Mark Sirower has already written plenty on that.[7] But this conversation around measuring does have ramifications for how you should think about synergies:

- **Synergy calculations are theoretical until you look "under the hood."** The investment bankers will deal in large swaths and work in broad terms to make the numbers work. That differs significantly from the specificity of integration planning, and why measuring to recalculate synergy targets is critical.
- **A target is only a motivational "stretch" if anchored to an empirical measure.** Stretch targets can only motivate teams if they're stretching what a team can actually attain.

- **The true cost of some synergies is not worth the cost to capture.** Just as you need to weigh how much value you expect a deal to return versus how much you're willing to pay, you must also weigh the potential cost of obtaining synergies versus the amount of value you expect them to generate.

- **Timing influences synergy capture.** As a rule, Year One synergies (other than procurement) never have any immediate synergy value because of the cost to capture, like paying for severance. Meanwhile, Year Two synergies are far more valuable than Year Three or Year Four synergies because building and demonstrating early momentum is vital to integration success. Moreover, synergy teams tend to backload their delivery of value to Year Three or later, which reflects over how much time they expect the necessary changes to occur *and* the results to subsequently materialize. This means that sequencing can also affect the cost to capture a synergy on the balance sheet and in the perceptual influence it has on other integration targets.

Evaluating the Feasibility of a Synergy Target

Before assigning a synergy target to an Integration Team, the IMO must ensure that the steps needed to achieve it—and the ramifications of achieving it—will actually render positive value. For example, if it costs more to let go of 20% of the unit than the present value of the savings we hope to achieve, is it even worth doing? Unlike setting motivational stretch targets, this is about making a "go/no-go" decision by considering the broader context of a proposed synergy source within the merged organization, a process that Sirower termed the "synergy matching principle."[8]

Your IMO can evaluate synergy targets effectively by creating a decision tree. This tree should trace each resultant decision and outcome required to achieve your proposed target. In the end, they'll have a series of branches that illustrate the effort needed to take action, as well as the "action cost" that all of it will take. Below, to illustrate just a fraction of this evaluative process, I've created a simplified example based on a relatively small (but very passionate) debate from the US Airways–American Airlines merger: what to do about warm nuts. Let me take you back in time.

The Warm Nuts Debate

In the airline industry, customer satisfaction is hard to achieve. Pitted against weather's regular unpredictability, there's never a guarantee of an on-time departure or arrival, much to passengers' chagrin. In the pre-merger days, delays plague American Airlines, a blight that ranks it below average in customer satisfaction in a troubled industry and relegates it to the ranks of the least-liked companies among American consumers (though Delta, United, and US Airways aren't far off).[9] Still, when it comes to its core demographic of business-class flyers, American Airlines prides itself on the quality of its in-flight service, amenities, facilities, and customer comfort—so much so, in fact, that pilots are empowered to hold flights for connecting passengers who are delayed.[10] As it turns out, American Airlines is so committed to its first-class experience that it is willing to risk added delays to accommodate a loyal customer core. And embodying that commitment are the warm nuts served to business and first-class passengers on every American Airlines flight—a trademark that the airline's leaders insist upon in integration planning talks with their former competitors.

For the US Airways team, whose only priority is ensuring flights leave on time, the question becomes: What would that take? Warming the nuts first requires an oven, a fixture that US Airways planes lack. Planes suffer from limited space, so outfitting an existing galley with the appliance will require an expansion that cuts into first-class seating. But shortchanging this high-margin section to serve a freebie *for that very section* is a no-go, meaning the first row will need to be pushed back. Available space is finite, so the economy section will have to be reconfigured at the expense of budget flyers' legroom. And the changed layout will need to be retrofitted across a fleet of thousands.

Then there are the staffing implications. You can't have an oven catch fire on a flight, so all US Airways flight attendants will need updated Occupational Safety and Health Administration training. Prior to that, the airline will need to revise its regulations and seek permission from the relevant unions, which will likely mean renegotiating contracts. Altogether, these considerations spin out a twisting tree that Figure 4.2, on the next page, only partially captures. Even more importantly, all told, the anticipated cost to preserve the tradition: tens of millions of dollars.

Uncovering Hidden Synergies

Data rooms are invaluable for due diligence and subsequent integration planning. While they might have been physical rooms back in the olden days, they typically function now as a shared platform between members of the merging entities, a convenient virtual space where all the documents and checklists come together for the due diligence. In recent years, these data rooms (sometimes known as "clean rooms," when they're given more restrictive access controls) have become even more effective at uncovering value thanks to the data analytics revolution: whether with the help of proprietary third-party providers or capabilities developed in-house, AI-powered data mining and analytics can digest vast quantities of customer data to predict future behavior, en route to more accurate appraisals, and even uncovering overlooked synergies.[11]

But even with super-powered capabilities, relying on these analyses alone is insufficient—not just for due diligence, but also for uncovering hidden synergies. You have to depart the data room. By relying on qualitative methods to supplement your quantitative understanding, you develop a much more three-dimensional, 360° perspective of the opportunities in front of you. Whether it's conducting employee interviews to find interpersonal synergies or talking with retail customers, as Procter & Gamble did, to learn that your acquisition target actually has a superior go-to-market,[12] a regimen of questions formed around the deal rationale can reveal unforeseen possibilities and help you avoid unexpected losses.

Figure 4.2   A simplified decision tree for warm nuts.

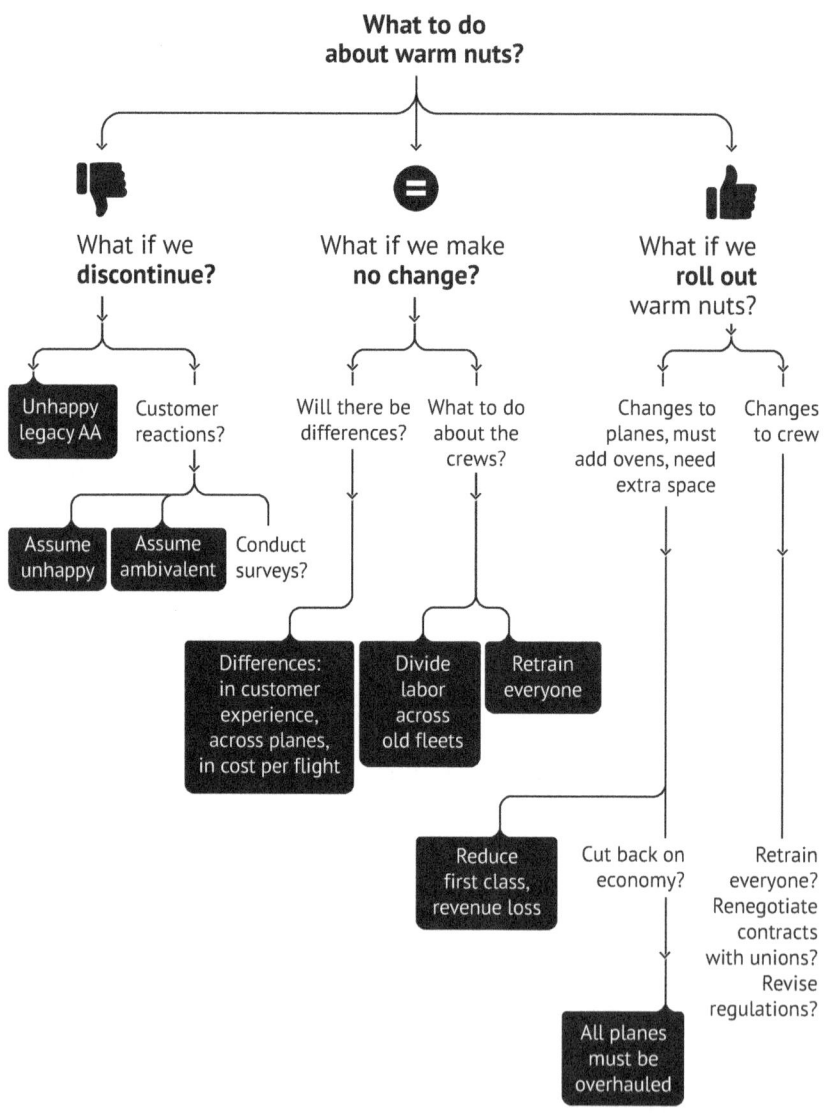

BASELINES: THE BEDROCK FOR INTEGRATION SUCCESS

This isn't the kind of book to lay out sample baseline calculations, but it's worth raising a few points that every member of Steerco, the IMO, and the Integration Teams should keep in mind going into integration planning. While baselines might seem like perfunctory calculations, throughout my time advising executives on integration matters, I've found that failure to establish baselines correlates with a failure to achieve desired goals. As a result, every leader should align their expectations around the baseline and tracking measurements that are appropriate for the deal.

The Fundamentals

A baseline is a comprehensive and detailed account of a company's financial and nonfinancial measures. It is a snapshot of each organization's pre-existing conditions *before the transaction*. The deal rationale should inform the depth, breadth, and focus of each baseline. Altogether, then, these essential pieces of data will inform how you turn your strategic aims into measurable goals that you can work toward through the integration. In this way, they can also help visualize your options for improvement, spot inconsistencies and overlaps, develop budgets and plans for the new organization—and measure the success of the deal.

You should take baseline measurements for both the acquiring company and the acquisition target across a range of assets. In her M&A tome, Alexandra Lajoux offers a helpful sample checklist which highlights the following:[13]

- Physical Assets (inventory, buildings, land, etc.)
- Financial Assets
- Intellectual Assets (patents, proprietary technology, etc.)

- Human Assets (not just headcounts, but what skills your workforce has, and concentrated where)
- Organizational Assets (systems and activities, like distribution channels)
- External Relationship Assets (customer service, labor relations, channel partners, etc.)

Who Drives Baseline Development?

While crunching the numbers often falls to consultants, Integration Teams should spearhead the development of their relevant baselines with guidance from the IMO. In terms of deal strategy, each team needs to develop its own baseline by working backwards from the individualized goals (end states) assigned to them as part of integration. Here, the IMO helps to translate the deal rationale into actionable items for each Integration Team. Tactically speaking, it's critical for the Integration Teams to drive the development process, as they will be responsible for measuring progress toward their assigned goals through integration. By empowering the teams to develop their own standards of measure (and thus establish their baselines), you increase both the likelihood that each team will be able to conduct their measurements effectively, and the motivation for each team to maintain necessary pace through integration planning and implementation.

In an ideal world, an acquirer would take stock of its assets prior to even making a bid, which would help streamline the baselining process for the Integration Teams. Of course, the point isn't so much to help the baselining process as it is to guide the organization toward an acquisition target that best suits its needs. As others have also advised, I've found that performing a SWOT analysis ("What are our Strengths, Weaknesses, Opportunities, and Threats?") is a simple way to accomplish this in a way that supports eventual baseline development.[14]

As for the acquisition target, the Integration Teams should still lead the development of baselines, but consultants can again be particularly helpful with gathering this data. My one word of caution is to ensure they do so with sensitivity. I've supported deals where members of the acquisition target perceived this data gathering like a raid, especially when the companies were former competitors, which could have seriously impacted the two sides' ability to come together, had the teams involved not taken care.

Baselines and the Uncertainty Principle

Earlier in this chapter, I mentioned the irony of measuring, and as the first instance of integration measuring, developing baselines will offer the same ironic challenge. The baseline will inform your teams' progress toward their synergy goals, so they need to be sufficiently detailed, but the teams need to produce them quickly so they can get working on achieving those goals—time pressure that limits how detailed those baselines can be. Once again, leaders must embrace the Uncertainty Principle.

Time is your perpetual rival: despite having a mindboggling amount of data you could collect and analyze, you simply don't have time to measure everything. Your teams must rely on the deal rationale (as appropriately relayed by the IMO) to determine the depth and breadth of their baseline. The nature of their goals should inform the scope of what they measure. Especially at the outset, Integration Teams must get real about what's relevant and what's extraneous and, depending on the time demands of the integration and how long it will take to obtain their measurements, aggressively prioritize the essentials from the "nice to haves." Perfect becomes the enemy of the good under integration's time pressures. To echo my McKinsey colleagues: "Balance the desire for baseline perfection with willingness to move quickly to create and capitalize on initiatives."[15]

THE INTEGRATION MASTERPLAN

Within the Parallel Process, Steerco and the IMO each hold distinct positions. Sitting atop the integration chain, Steerco determines the set of principles that comprise the overarching strategy to realize the deal rationale. The IMO, meanwhile, deals in the *tactics* meant to deploy that strategy in tangible ways. That is the masterplan.

Through the masterplan, the IMO structures the entirety of the integration's implementation. It documents the priorities, timing, and structure of everything we've discussed in this chapter thus far and then some—quite literally the entire integration. That means it is a multilayered, group effort between the IMO and Integration Teams, as well as a living document. While its depth and precision will not automatically guarantee the integration's success, its sloppiness could create additional (and otherwise preventable) roadblocks.

Others have dedicated entire chapters to the granularities of integration masterplans, like Scott Whitaker in his *Mergers & Acquisitions Integration Handbook*.[16] For our purposes, here is a checklist for the essentials that any masterplan should aim to do:

- Confirm the overall direction of the merger and drive the integration effort.
- Establish a priority list of major integration requirements, ranked according to their criticality and the desired timing of their results.
- Set out, by team, key outcome measurements and timing expectations for team deliverables.
- Detail how Integration Team leaders will interact with business unit and functional leaders to drive required planning efforts.

- Identify key interdependencies and illustrate how the individual merger initiatives fit together.
- Identify the critical path and set out a cadence of meeting and communication processes.

But it's worth getting into a few specifics. Whenever I work on a masterplan with an integration manager—usually starting with the acquiring CEO and then the IMO Leader—I make sure they consider the following questions.

What's the Purpose of the Masterplan?

In every deal, the masterplan starts as a high-level snapshot that sketches the vision for the goals of the integration. What is the strategic rationale for the deal in its most fundamental sense, and what are the initial goals based on that rationale? From that initial snapshot, the masterplan should evolve over the course of the integration to reflect the progress that's been made, as well as the most updated version of the integration goals (as they can change over time). What form that takes—and what level of detail and control is required—depends on the specifics of your deal.

What Level of Detail Is Required?

As always, it depends, but in most cases, you'll want to make your masterplan rigorous, precisely detailed, and very tightly controlled (by the IMO, with critical oversight by Steerco). In broad strokes, the IMO will use the masterplan to set the schedule for each Integration Team, coordinate their activities, and (co)determine the means to measure their respective performance. For especially complex integrations like US Airways–American Airlines, the plan might also identify goals and milestones beyond the point when the IMO is discontinued and long-term integration goals (for, e.g., systems and cultural integration) become central BU responsibilities. Though it usually takes some time to get there, this could mean detail at the level of *several thousand* integration tasks stretching over three or four years.

Let me highlight just a few from the US Airways–American Airlines merger. There was a central debate around network optimization versus customer service: do you allow pilots to hold a plane for an incoming connecting flight, as American Airlines had, or do you phase out the policy, as the US Airways side staunchly argued? Pilot callsigns: do you integrate all the pilots onto a shared designation for cultural integration, or do you allow the US Airways pilots to keep their old callsigns, despite phasing out the rest of the airline's branding? Terminal layouts: how do you (re)arrange the layout, for example, of Boston Logan Airport, whose Terminal B had been split between American Airlines and US Airways, with a parking lot in the middle? In each of these cases, just like the warm nuts story above, Integration Leaders had to play out an entire chain of logic and decisions to determine what made the most sense in light of the deal rationale and base business.

This level of detail is extremely useful in cases where the merging companies don't have strong project management cultures, when you need a high degree of central control to minimize risk, and when you need multiple teams to interact and coordinate closely to create desired value. Ultimately, with so many variables at play and so much data coming from all directions, integration leadership owe it to themselves to create as detailed a map as possible, one they can use to find the way even amid the chaos and confusion that will likely come.

Sometimes, though, you won't need this level of detail and control. In a deal driven primarily by business-as-usual, for example, you might only need a top-level path of major milestones. Leaders with prior integration experience or organizations with dedicated integration staff and a tested set of integration processes will also tend to streamline the master-planning effort (practice may not make perfect, but it does build stronger integration "muscles"). In the end, the determination should come down to the specs of your merger and the intensity of your integration.

Who Controls the Plan?

In most cases, the IMO controls the plan. That said, in recent years, companies have been investing in entities like a Transformation Office that maintain dedicated staff to oversee transformation initiatives, including integration. Organizations with these capabilities sometimes choose to include a member of the Transformation Office on the IMO or, particularly if the deal is relatively small or simpler to integrate, the Transformation Office might handle the bulk of the traditional IMO work. In that case, the Transformation Office would essentially own the masterplan. Either way, entrusting the masterplan to a central body helps maintain control across all the Integration Teams and makes it easier to sequence interdependencies (e.g., when workstreams require another stream cross-functionally to accomplish their goals, like needing IT to acquire licensing for new software).

What Actually Goes into Developing the Masterplan?

As team leaders and the IMO work to validate baseline measurements and their target goals, they should look to accomplish a few things:

- Quantify baseline in sufficient detail to set targets, plan, and measure performance.
- Ensure key leaders agree on their baseline(s). They should concur that the sum of the "pre-merger" components, before synergy effects are considered, is (sufficiently) accurate and reflects all relevant planned investments and corresponding returns from the

pre-merger organizations. (Note that there will be too many moving parts for these baseline measurements to be "audit quality.")

- Ensure consistent definitions, timeframes, and allocation approaches across companies and organizational units.
- Set up a process to verify baseline allocations are comprehensive and do not overlap—so it's clear who is doing what.
- Structure budgets so they can be cut and reconciled easily in multiple dimensions, for example, by the Integration Team, organizational unit, or senior executive. (And keep budget reallocations to an absolute minimum!)
- Ensure baselines can be reconciled against existing budgets, plans, and future management accounts.
- Determine the timeframe to achieve your targeted numbers, with particular focus on Year One. (Too often, companies project synergies by Years Three or Four, but these synergies have much more value in Year One—because it's after Year One that deals are deemed successful or not.)
- Assess the baseline versus the actual—how well you're doing relative to overall levels of headcounts and budgets for a given group of people. Pay attention to the gap between the baseline and the final number.
- Track the softer, more performance-oriented metrics that relate to the deal rationale.

Best Practices for the Masterplan

In addition to these key questions, here are a few best practices as you start preparing your masterplan:

- **Develop early and revise often.** Masterplans are living things. You have to keep adjusting your plan as the landscape shifts, the path becomes clearer, and the obstacles and opportunities more apparent. But keep in mind that you don't need to start at the level of thousands of lines of instruction: often it begins with a simple "mud map," a top-level timeline to set constraints and help speed planning later.

- **Have a clear reporting architecture.** A good masterplan provides a clear architecture for reporting the information to the people it matters to most. Steerco and senior management, for example, should get regular updates on progress toward major milestones, while individual teams should receive details on the activities that drive those milestones. And, because some integration efforts are interdependent and will naturally impact others, individual teams should also receive updates on what other teams are doing and deciding. This means that a good plan lets information flow across these levels to minimize data entry, while reporting occurs at different levels of aggregation.

- **Establish a regular tracking cadence.** The IMO must keep Integration Teams on track to ensure they're measuring progress regularly and in the right way. Teams should regularly provide updates to the IMO and attend joint IMO meetings to learn about each other's progress. Integration meetings often occur every two weeks.

- **Integrate the integration.** To streamline things as much as possible, develop the structure of your masterplan top down, level by level, to prevent duplication and ensure that nothing falls through the cracks. I've found that a top-level timeline is the best starting point to provide an integrated view of the key milestones everyone needs to accomplish.

- **Automate.** Given the world we live in, there's no need to do everything by hand. Digital tools, including AI-powered assets, can help automate reporting to identify the tasks that are late or off the mark and highlight critical interdependencies across workstreams.

BRINGING IT ALL TOGETHER

To close this chapter, allow me to synthesize this convoluted dance between Steerco, the IMO, and the Integration Teams into a few simplified steps:

1. Steerco aligns the IMO on its goals for the deal and its main heuristics for synergy capture.
2. The IMO sets initial targets and assigns them to individual Integration Teams.
3. The Integration Teams develop their measures and take baselines to validate and/or refine their assigned targets.
4. Informed by this data (provided by the IMO), Steerco sets and approves overall synergy targets (by, e.g., business unit and function).
5. Based on the designated synergy targets, Integration Teams design their individual integration plans.
6. The IMO validates and/or refines those plans, folding them into their broader masterplan and using them to create a tracking cadence.
7. Steerco reviews the plans with the IMO, implementing any desired change (if needed) before giving approval.
8. The IMO assigns the approved plans back to the Integration Teams, who ready them for implementation by the "business as usual" leaders.
9. Once implementation begins after Day One, the IMO tracks progress against the plans, stepping in to make changes or revise targets as needed.

As I learned from Niamh Dawson, she and her Boston Consulting Group colleagues refer to this as the "W approach," based on how they've helpfully visualized it.[17] During my time with McKinsey, we adopted a similar kind of methodology, which looked something like Figure 4.3.

Figure 4.3 Integration planning flow.

Source: Adapted from Daniel Friedman, Axel Reinaud, Chris Barrett, and Niamh Dawson, "Six Essentials for Achieving Postmerger Synergies," Boston Consulting Group, March 17, 2017, https://www.bcg.com/publications/2017/postmerger-integration-six-essentials-for-achieving-postmerger-synergies (accessed April 23, 2025).

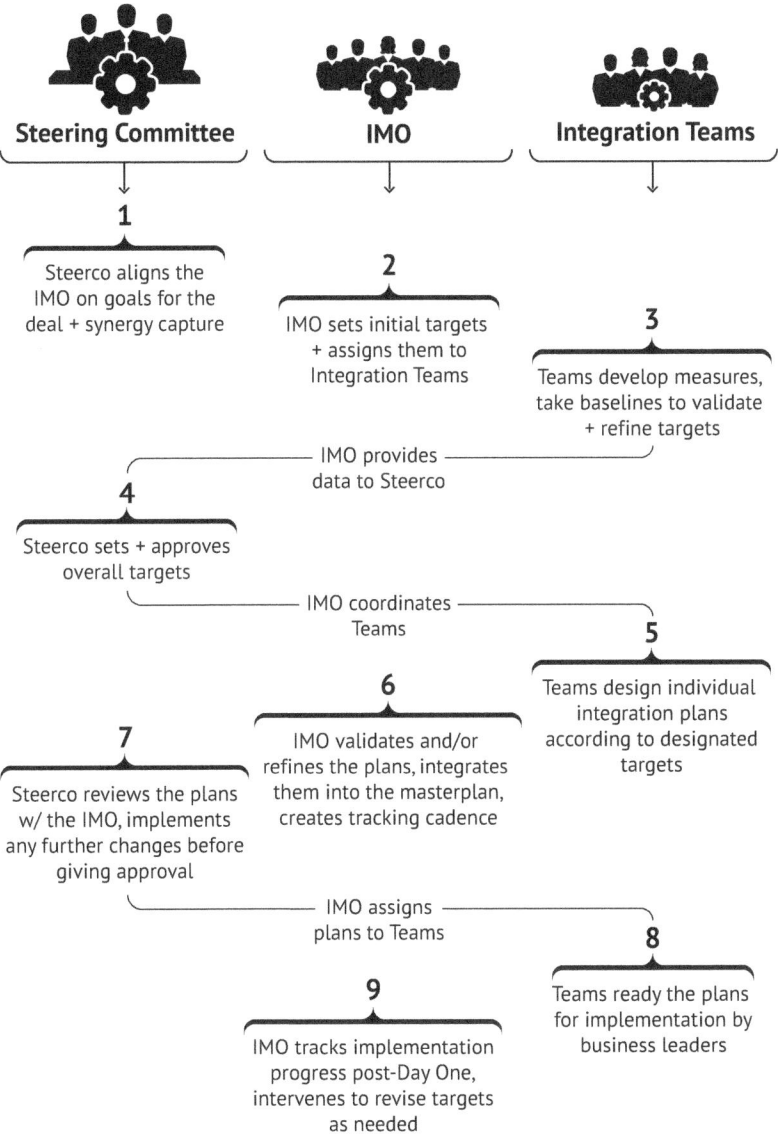

Steering Committee   **IMO**   **Integration Teams**

1
Steerco aligns the IMO on goals for the deal + synergy capture

2
IMO sets initial targets + assigns them to Integration Teams

3
Teams develop measures, take baselines to validate + refine targets

IMO provides data to Steerco

4
Steerco sets + approves overall targets

IMO coordinates Teams

5
Teams design individual integration plans according to designated targets

6
IMO validates and/or refines the plans, integrates them into the masterplan, creates tracking cadence

7
Steerco reviews the plans w/ the IMO, implements any further changes before giving approval

IMO assigns plans to Teams

8
Teams ready the plans for implementation by business leaders

9
IMO tracks implementation progress post-Day One, intervenes to revise targets as needed

ACTION ITEMS IN REVIEW

- **Don't place false confidence in due diligence**—you won't know what the reality is until you own the acquisition and can look "under the hood."
- **Proactively measure baselines and progress toward target synergies**—data-gathering capacity will not automatically produce integration results.
- **Have Integration Teams calculate baselines and determine appropriate measuring systems by working backward from initial synergy targets**—and then refine synergy targets according to the baseline "real."
- **Empower the Teams to set baselines early**—they have to determine the right balance between depth, breadth, and speed depending on their targets, while rigorously determining what degree of detail is a "must have" versus a "nice to have."
- **Ensure that synergy targets should return more value than the "action cost"** associated with obtaining them.
- **Empower the IMO to create a tight, detailed integration masterplan** that secures Integration Teams within a regular tracking cadence.

CHAPTER FIVE

COMMUNICATING BEYOND THE ANNOUNCEMENT: SETTING THE NARRATIVE FOR YOUR INTEGRATION

T he day has finally come. After a grueling few weeks in the trenches with the investment bankers, lawyers, your most trusted advisors and lieutenants, as well as key players from the other side, you can finally announce to the world your plans for something transformational. The wording has been thoughtfully sewn together and meticulously tweaked dozens of times with input from both companies. With this, you formally proclaim the start of the next chapter.

The announcement looms large for a reason. It's an attention grabber that quite literally makes the headlines. It's the first opportunity to put forth the case for these once-separate organizations to become one. It's a tone setter, an excitement generator, a proclamation of grand intent. But the announcement is really only the beginning—or, more accurately, it's only one (albeit important) part within a broader communications effort that will span the entirety of the integration to come.

While it may be the starting *bang*, the initial surge it kicks off won't last the whole race without other messages of encouragement along the way—as well as some guideposts to make sure you actually reach the finish line. That's why, as HR and Transformation leads will no doubt tell you, town halls, coffee chats, newsletters, and other forms of outreach are essential to any serious integration. But, however important these elements are (and they absolutely are), they can only do so much without something else to pull them all together.

To take your communications from a long to-do list of communiqués and events to a cohesive, nuanced, and value-generative effort, you need to craft a unifying narrative. This is the master narrative for your entire deal—in effect, the articulation of your deal rationale, and consequently the articulation of the "whys" behind everything you're undertaking through integration. But this, of course, presents a problem: what if your ultimate intent is sensitive and must be kept under wraps? You can't exactly risk losing the competitive advantage from a novel insight or prematurely tip your hand to layoffs that might be coming down the road. The answer, I've found, requires careful consideration of your stakeholders and the nuanced stakes they have in your deal.

This chapter is all about the master narrative: what it is, how you formulate it, and how you might deploy it to keep your integration's focus channeled in the direction you want it to go. It is *not* about the specific kinds of communications (like town halls and memos) that more technical playbooks often cover. I'll begin by making the case for the narrative approach and outlining the major components it entails. Then, I'll home in on the core of your narrative, the primary message you want to convey every time you communicate with a stakeholder, whether internal or external. Next is how to tailor that message according to each stakeholder group. Along the way, I'll walk you through how I work with leaders to take stock of the needs of these groups, the individualized interests they might have in your deal, and how to address those interests through your communications. After highlighting an easy way to build credibility—promoting the process you're undertaking—I'll close with a few words on timing and cadence.

STRUCTURING YOUR COMMUNICATION: THE GUIDING QUESTIONS

For all the emphasis that data gets in our increasingly analytical world, there's no denying the power of a good story. We certainly understand this from a marketing perspective (how else would Clydesdales make for a good beer commercial?), and with the boom of narrative-style presentations like TED in the 2010s and onward, more audiences than ever have been exposed to storytelling as a persuasive form.

As for the business case, we've certainly come a long way since *Harvard Business Review* interviewed screenwriter Robert McKee (of *Forrest Gump* and *Toy Story* fame) about the power of storytelling for CEOs back in 2003.[1] Now, we understand that stories can have even more staying power than compelling data framed without a compelling narrative—perhaps up to 22 times more.[2] Studies tell us that they're effective precisely because they can engage audience members both emotionally and logically,[3] maybe even producing specific chemicals in the brain related to empathy, emotional regulation, and memory formation.[4]

We also better understand what it takes to craft a powerful story. As I've learned over my career as an educator, it shares quite a bit of overlap with the essentials of good writing. I like to think in terms of a series of questions: What is it that I'm trying to say? Who is my audience? How should I communicate my point to them? And why is any of it important?

M&A communications also follow these basic storytelling fundamentals. While you might not be making a direct argument as you would with a TED talk or presentation, the overlap is clear: you want to effectively convey a series of messages in ways that resonate with your audience. It's not enough just to put something out there and call it a day, nor is it particularly useful to frame things in a way that only you and those closest to you can appreciate. Weaving together a compelling narrative—a good story—requires tailoring how and what you're communicating, depending on who you're talking to.

Thankfully, you can achieve this by asking yourself a few simple questions:

- **Who do you need to address?** This is the first question you should consider, even before you think about what you're going to communicate. From customers, vendors, partners, investors, and employees (from each company), you have countless stakeholders who will be affected by your deal, and each needs to be addressed in their own way.

- **Why do you need to address them?** This isn't meant to sound dismissive. Rather, it's about getting to the core of how each stakeholder relates to the deal—how they might be affected by it, what it could mean for them—to help you pinpoint the central elements that concern them, both positive and less so. Channel partners, for example, might wonder how the nature of your business together will change; employees, meanwhile, might worry about what the deal will mean for their jobs.

- **What is it that you need to convey to them?** This is where you solidify the meat of that message—what different stakeholders need to know. For those channel partners, perhaps nothing will change (which is still a very important message to convey). For some employees, meanwhile, perhaps they will lose their jobs. Identifying the most important takeaways, however, doesn't mean you need to convey that message all at once—not to mention that regulatory and strategy concerns will likely prevent you from doing so. Instead, it's about developing a very specific understanding of how each party may be affected by the deal.

- **How will you convey it?** This is less about the medium you'll use to convey your message than it is about the tone you'll strike with each stakeholder group. It's typically in your interest to frame your message in a way that is both authentic and mindful of the audience's position. If you're telling your channel partners that nothing will change, your message should be reassuring. If layoffs are likely coming, even if you can't tell your employees yet, your messages to them shouldn't be disingenuous—that everything is going to be great.

- **When (how frequently) will you convey it?** These communications aren't a one-time thing. In fact, stakeholders' desire for information will verge on insatiable in the face of uncertainty. From process updates to major progress reports, you and your communications team will need to create a structure for communicating with your different stakeholders around key milestones. This includes mapping out when you can release critical pieces of information through the integration lifecycle.

While an approach as simple as this won't win you a Peabody Award, it can help you start to think like a storyteller. And it's this way of thinking that will allow you to transform communications around your deal into a narrative in both senses of the word—not just an account of what's happening, but a way of "understanding a situation or series of events

Figure 5.1   A narrative framework for integration communication.

1. Craft the Narrative Working from your deal rationale

2. Tailor the Message According to your stakeholder audiences

3. Promote the Process Communicate transparently about what you're doing

4. Calibrate the Cadence Around key milestones (according to stakeholder)

that reflects and promotes a particular point of view or set of values." Or, in less Merriam-Webster terms, *how you want people to understand your deal*, ideally before they have the chance to jump to their own conclusions. Figure 5.1 channels this thinking into an actionable framework for integration communications, which starts with the strength and tenor of the message at the core of your narrative.

CRAFTING THE CORE

A communication strategy is nothing without a message to communicate. This might sound obvious, but it's worth taking a moment to think about what really constitutes a "message." An announcement, update, or progress report is not a message, though these are critical things to communicate as part of your strategy. Rather, your message is of a higher order, something that motivates and unifies those individual instances of communication.

Your message is what you want your audience to come away with, in service of your ultimate goals—in this case, why you're doing the deal, to the extent you can share. While each individual piece of communication will have its own function—a progress report, for example, might be designed to both update and motivate a specific audience—every communication should also serve to reinforce understanding of the deal rationale.

This kind of narrative communication shares some overlap with strategic communications. To successfully implement corporate strategy, it's not enough for companies to adopt a "tactical, short-term approach."[5] Instead, they must also convey a longer-term strategic direction through integrated communications that "sound like they are coming from the same place leading in the same direction."[6] One way to do this is to continually link strategic decisions to the organization's purpose or goal,[7] which serves to contextualize its actions within a goal-oriented narrative. In fact, without this narrative-setting approach to strategic communications, the makeup of a company's strategy risks falling quickly out of sight. MIT Sloan's Donald Sull and colleagues found that, among executives and middle managers charged with executing strategy, only 28% could list even three of their strategic priorities.[8] (And if that's the case at the top, imagine how muddled things are in the rest of the organization.)

As with strategy, the core of your message keeps your organization focused on the priority integration items while curtailing tangential speculation and misguided debates. In practice, that means every time you release a statement about your deal's progress, you tie it back to why you're doing it in the first place, even if the way you convey that varies depending on audience.

Setting the Narrative: Your Story's First-Mover Advantage

You've certainly heard of the first-mover advantage sometime in your career. Particularly with the explosion of startup culture and the democratization of entrepreneurial innovation, it's come back into vogue because it posits that the first player into a new space has an inherent competitive edge over its competitors. Now, plenty of research has shown this isn't a hard and fast truth—after all, if it were a guarantee of success, Netscape might still be the browser of choice. But there is an air of truth to it: sometimes the early bird does get the worm, and being the first on the scene does yield its advantages, provided the conditions are right.[9]

As it turns out, narratives seem to work in much the same way. In the 1980s, Jerome Bruner, one of the most influential psychologists of the century, began developing a theory that revolutionized how we understand human understanding. In short, we seem predisposed to do so through stories: in order to make sense of our past, history, and the world around us, we connect moments into a storyline from which we can draw a kind of logic.

Critically, the earliest versions of such stories are particularly influential. In what he called "narrative accrual,"[10] he observed how people, both individually and societally, take existing stories and build on them over time, until those stories become like a myth imbued with a certain kind of meaning (think of George Washington refusing to chop down the cherry tree, and how we understand his virtue as quintessentially American). Although aspects of the story might change over time, the underlying narrative was set from the outset. It's like the Anchoring Effect for stories: because we have a cognitive bias to over-rely on the first piece of information made available to us,[11] it's often the first version of a story we hear that sets the tone (the narrative) for our understanding.

This has two closely related implications for integration communications. First, if you're the first to set the narrative, yours will likely be the one that catches on (provided you, your Integration Leaders, and leadership throughout your organization continue to reinforce it). Alternatively, if you don't set the narrative, others will fill the silence on your behalf. Let's consider a few examples.

In 2021, Canadian Pacific and Kansas City Southern announced a merger poised to be one of the most significant in recent memory. With their union, the combined railroad lines would run coast-to-coast in Canada and down through the continental United States well into Mexico, making it the first line to operate across North America.[12] The internal goal was ambitious, as the expanded system could have the potential to circumvent the Panama Canal, in addition to the many scale and operational benefits. But this wasn't something they could announce. Instead, the announcement proudly declared that they were creating "the first U.S.-Mexico-Canada rail network … that will deliver dramatically expanded market reach for … customers, provide new competitive transportation options, and support North American economic growth."[13]

Outsiders quickly began spinning their own narratives. Was it about the locomotives they were using? Maybe they needed to improve their cash-flow? Competitors also took the chance to pitch in their two cents: clearly these rails weren't doing well and had taken this path out of desperation! When I met with the company's top leaders, consequently, we worked on making the core message even more consistent, concise, and unwavering: "We're looking to gain access to Mexican markets and accelerate transportation of goods through the Midwest and Canada." Like a mantra, they were to recite this one sentence—even in the dentist's chair, if they had to.

There will be no shortage of external speculation about your merger's motivations, and not just from the analysts. There are plenty of others who may be impacted by the deal that will also be looking for answers. Employees across both organizations will feel particularly vulnerable. Without proper clarity, they will create their own narratives or otherwise latch onto the most compelling ones available to them, whether true or not. After all, when a new circumstance arises, people want to understand what it will mean for them. If they face ambiguity, phenomenologists argue, they will engage in "sensemaking," a process that "involves turning circumstances into a situation that is comprehended explicitly in words and that serves as a springboard into action," or one by which they "search for meaning, settle for plausibility, and move on."[14] In other words, just like

Bruner theorized, *they create their own narrative.* This behavior is amplified in groups, which leads to the destructive rumor mill that has plagued many a deal that looked strong at close.

The Risk of Setting the Wrong Narrative

Yet even beyond quelling the rumor mill, crafting and sticking to a core message that reflects your deal rationale will help you stay focused on what's most important. Some leaders have learned this the hard way. During one of my assignments as an advisor, I had the opportunity to meet with the CEO of an acquiring company to help him strategize for his first address after the announcement of the deal. The obvious priority was to clearly articulate why he was doing the deal, but no less important was connecting that rationale to other key decisions the reporters were bound to ask him about. One of those questions would surely be about the leadership of the combined company. After much back and forth, we agreed that absolutely, under no circumstances, could he say, "We'll take the best of both." And yet, under the bright lights of the press conference, that's exactly what happened.

Going for the "best of both" approach isn't inherently an issue. One of the first internal communiqués that P&G released after it announced its merger with Gillette declared that it would be "fielding the best team" across both organizations. Despite the procedural difficulties and the anxiety it produced among some legacy P&Gers, the decision fit well with the leaders' goal to make the deal "a once in a lifetime opportunity [to] upgrad[e] the quality of the combined company."[15] It communicated to Gillette's best that they had the chance to prove themselves, that they weren't unwanted goods.

The issue was that my CEO friend had other priorities in mind for the deal. Thoroughly evaluating talent from both companies would take months of valuable time that he wasn't sure he had. Even more to the point, he already intended to keep most of his people in place. His subconscious desire to settle everyone's anxieties was understandable, but his answer needed to stick to the core message. Instead, in that moment, one slip was all it took to commit him to a long evaluation period that cost the company three months before he made his appointments.

TAILORING THE MESSAGE

A deal is about much more than the two companies coming together. The spotlight may be on you, but there's a whole cast of players for whom this transaction, even if it's relatively small, is potentially a big deal. Deals like this mean change, a tricky fact of life that many people need time and structure to adjust to. Everyone with a stake in your business, whether fellow organizations or individuals, will be wondering some version of, "What does this mean *for me*?" Analysts might fret over how the combined companies will cut costs that have spiraled out of control. Customers will focus on how the merger will affect service. And then there's the consumer activist groups demanding to know how you'll address the environmental issues that have plagued the acquired business.

The intensity of this wondering may vary by party, but each merits your thoughtful and early consideration. Even a quarter century ago, a group of "master acquirers," assembling for a Harvard Business School roundtable on making mergers succeed, recognized the importance of addressing stakeholder concerns early in the process.[16] In fact, acknowledging them early is an essential step in maintaining the base business, one of the major truths I highlighted in Chapter One: if you want to keep all your primary functions running smoothly, you'll need to loop in the various parties that those functions depend on. You might not be able to get into all the specifics, but simply acknowledging their concerns expresses your awareness of their position and your intent to act when it's feasible. This in turn allows them to stay ahead—if only by a little—of the innumerable questions and boundless speculation that M&A so often produces.

To best increase the odds of integration success, you'll need to consider both your *internal* and *external* stakeholders. Unsurprisingly, your internal stakeholders are your employees. The challenge, however, lies in treating them not as a collective, but instead analyzing how different subgroups across *both* the acquired and acquiring organizations might be affected by the deal in different ways. Appropriately addressing external audiences, meanwhile, presents a different kind of challenge: here, you're identifying the many ways your company engages with the outside world, including through the pieces you're now acquiring. Let's take a look at some of the factors you should consider when developing your communication strategy for each of these large stakeholder categories (see Figure 5.2).

Figure 5.2 Identifying and communicating with stakeholders.

External Stakeholders	Internal Stakeholders
Identify via the Deal Rational	**Look to Both Sides**
• Which external groups will be impacted by the deal, and in what way(s)? • How does each group relate to the organization? • Which will likely face the most disruption?	• Who can you not afford to lose (the "flight risks")? Why? • Who is most likely to be affected or disrupted by the deal, and in what way(s)?
Tailoring the Message	**Tailoring the Message**
• How will the deal change your organization (relative to the stakeholder)? • What does that change mean for this specific stakeholder?	• Why are they important to the organization? To the integration? • What does that change mean for this specific stakeholder? If you can't provide full disclosure right away, what can you disclose?

External Stakeholders

Overseeing a major transaction, you'll quickly be reminded in no uncertain terms just how many external stakeholders you have. Clearly, anyone that interfaces directly with your business, whether that's customers, distributors, partners, vendors, or otherwise, is a stakeholder. But so are analysts, investors, regulatory bodies, and even voices in the media. In fact, when you think about the reach of your announcement, you could even consider the public at large as a passive stakeholder. That's the challenge of tailoring your message for outside audiences: there are seemingly countless groups to consider, each of which has a distinct set of concerns, interests, and perspectives. Cross-cutting their differences, however, are two questions that all of them want you to answer.

I mentioned the first question earlier in this chapter: "What does this deal—and the changes it will produce—mean *for me*?" In answering this question, you're tailoring your message in targeted ways that clearly address the nature of their stake in your deal. Take Amazon's 2017 acquisition of Whole Foods. The online retailer had already put skin in the grocery game with Amazon Fresh, including brick-and-mortar stores,[17] so while much of the narrative homed in on cost-structure efficiencies,[18] there was now a long list of producers wondering who they would be selling to, and how.

Sometimes, local communities will want to know what a deal might mean for them. This was certainly the case with the American Airlines deal, since the airline was one of the largest employers around Dallas. Consequently, the IMO's communications lead started interfacing directly with some of the area's major newspapers, which began publishing weekly columns on the deal's progress. While the updates were detail-oriented, the consistent message was one of reassurance: don't worry, we're staying in Dallas.

The second question aims more toward the heart of the deal: "Who are they?"[19] (i.e., Who are *you*?) This isn't just about whether the acquired company will be folded into the acquirer and rebranded. It's about identity: What are your values, and what will you do in light of this transaction? It's the most obvious signpost for the narrative you want to set for your deal.

The announcement is the most visible example of this kind of messaging. When Microsoft announced its acquisition of LinkedIn in 2016, CEO Satya Nadella grandly proclaimed it was about the two companies joining together to "empower every person and organization on the planet."[20] His counterparts bolstered that message, with LinkedIn Chairman and cofounder Reid Hoffman declaring it a "re-founding moment" for the professional network, one that CEO Jeff Weiner concurred offered "a chance to also change the way the world works."[21] Here, the public is the external stakeholder, and the message to them is clear: through this deal, we're making your work easier by better empowering and connecting you and your organization.

But if we think of the announcement as just one example of external communication (one directed to the public), we should also address the identity question with every other outside stakeholder. Taking this perspective, we can begin to see how your answers to these two questions can work in harmony toward your deal's goals. Let's return to Amazon and Whole Foods. The announcement focused on "bringing the highest quality, experience, convenience and innovation to our customers," said the grocer's co-founder and CEO John Mackey,[22] but outreach to producers surely communicated two additional messages. First: we're committed to operational excellence, and this deal will significantly reduce costs ("Who are you?"). And second: that means we can stock and sell more of your goods ("What does this mean for me?").

Over the years, I've also found it helpful to engage audiences in two-way dialogue to increase their buy-in and ensure they're receiving your message in the ways you intend. Customer advisory panels are a great example of this, since they help stakeholders stay engaged and receive helpful feedback. In fact, for the Merck–Schering-Plough deal, pulling together panels of physicians proved one of the most valuable pieces of the communications strategy. On the face of it, these panels allowed us to ask a critical stakeholder group how they were receiving and understanding messages from the companies about what the deal was meant to accomplish, as well as what the merger meant to them—valuable insight we could use to tailor the message around how the companies wanted to improve what they were offering to doctors. At the same time, these panels also helped spread the message to other stakeholder groups at a grassroots level, as these physicians would then go and talk with healthcare administrators, patients, hospital executives, and so on.

Internal Stakeholders

Your internal stakeholders also deserve personalized communications about the deal. I'm sure this isn't news to you. Nearly every leader I've encountered knows they need the buy-in and focus from people in their organization to make something as challenging as integration go as hoped—and that it will take a real communications effort to make that happen. Even scholars can agree on this, despite the hazy impression the literature gives off: while they're not so clear on what to do, there is at least agreement that how you communicate the deal with your employees can significantly affect their experience of the integration.[23]

At the same time, I've often found that those in charge of internal communications are more preoccupied with the means of communicating than determining specifically who they should be targeting. But simply adopting different tactics will only get you so far. This disconnect becomes clearer and clearer every time I teach Harvard's executive education program on M&A. Each year, within a group of 80 executives (from Vice Presidents and Integration Directors to lawyers and bankers), the vast majority agree that directly engaging employees through town halls and webinars was crucial in earning their buy-in, but most of them still acknowledge that they faced people problems through integration.

In this section, I want to impart two major takeaways. First, make sure you're keeping the employees of both companies in mind. Second, take the time to identify the employee subgroups that the deal will most affect. As always, the throughline is to let the deal rationale be your guide in determining what groups might be impacted in different ways.

Target Both Organizations

Let's start at the broadest level: make sure you pay attention to employees on both sides of the deal. Go-to materials on integration overwhelmingly prioritize employees in the acquired organization because of the instability from being on the "losing" side. In Chapter One, for example, I mentioned a popular 2024 study that showed roughly a third of acquired startup employees left within the first year of the acquisition.[24] This is just one piece among many that, while certainly revealing, has contributed to the sense that disruption is felt more often and more powerfully in the acquisition target.[25] But there's good reason to believe that it's more than just the acquired side that experiences the "merger syndrome," the complex emotional phenomenon that people throughout merging organizations face as uncertainty disrupts reality within their organizations.[26]

In fact, employees in the acquiring organization also have good reason to feel anxious. After Dell Technologies acquired the data storage company EMC in 2016, it cut over 2,000 of its own jobs in supply chain, marketing, and other areas of overlap with its acquisition.[27] The situation was even more dire for HP following its deal with Compaq: between the complications it faced from the transaction and market conditions, the acquiring company decided to lay off around 8,000 of its employees (in addition to thousands at Compaq).[28] And sometimes it's the anticipation of change, a paradigm shift, or a shakeup of the status quo that causes alarm:[29] for some P&Gers, just the announcement of the deal with Gillette was enough to liken it to the day John F. Kennedy was assassinated—and that was well before there were hints of a "field the best team" approach.[30]

Fissures within your existing organization pose serious threats to your base business, which in turn will threaten to obstruct integration success. I'll elaborate more on this in Chapter Six on Day One priorities, but in short, increased expenditures related to the deal, delayed realization of synergy value in virtually all areas but procurement, and anxieties churned up by integration decisions (and speculation) require a counterbalancing force that your base business must provide. In order to achieve that, you have to actively engage your existing employees and acknowledge their involvement in this uneasy process.

Employee Subgroups

Employees are not a monolith. This is something many of us know, but when you're trying to address so much changing territory and anxiety, it can sadly fall to the wayside. Internal announcements sometimes stay at the level of A company or X business unit when more granularity around role, region, tenure, or other marker is what's needed. But I'm not asking you to do the impossible and identify every individual subgroup. Rather, let the deal rationale guide you to the groups that are most central to the critical path.

For example, who are the employees you can't afford to lose? Given how significant a concern talent retention is for the majority of dealmakers,[31] it's critical that you identify early on the influencers who might be feeling the most precarious. In an airline merger, for example, that might be the people who know the linear programs and develop the flight schedules for the whole fleet given the tradeoffs of fuel consumption. Or maybe it's the so-called staff sergeants, those with pivotal roles below the senior executives—for IBM–Lenovo, they were the ones managing the supply chain relationships with Microsoft and Intel. Reaching out to these valuable "flight risks" with messages that contextualize their importance to the new organization can supplement (though not replace) incentive packages, increasing your odds of meeting your synergy goals.

There's a similar logic around maintaining the base business. Employees at risk of being eliminated understandably tend to lose momentum as their anxieties increase (and as they look for new jobs). This can impact your base business at the time you need it to pull through the most. Being transparent with those at risk of being eliminated about the unfolding integration and its potential ramifications for them, as well as opening channels for them to voice their concerns, may also serve to alleviate tension and maintain morale.

There may be certain "single-issue" employee groups—folks with a unique concern in the deal—who are also worth addressing. For US Airways, it was the people in Pittsburgh, those still connected to the old Allegheny Airlines I mentioned in Chapter One. Discussing this issue now, so many years separated from the politics and emotion, it might sound like a simple issue to resolve. By bringing American Airlines into the fold, the combined airline now had access to a huge facility in Dallas that outstripped the legacy center in nearly every way. But the people in Pittsburgh really cared about that place. They took pride in it, even as a "legacy" facility, precisely because it represented a treasured legacy within the airline's history. This meant that they were willing to lobby *hard* to maintain it. As a result, it took a dedicated effort to communicate with them, not only to acknowledge their concerns, but also to remind them of the reason behind the deal. At the end of the day, the narrative was all about scaling up, and that meant letting go of a piece of history to land a hub better suited for the future.

PROMOTING THE PROCESS

Now let's focus on a way to lend your narrative further credibility. So far, our conversation has looked largely to storytelling strategies: distilling your message, considering your audience, and delivering in ways that resonate. These matters of form all serve to realize your ultimate function in landing the deal smoothly through integration. But a narrative loses its strength when the audience finds reason to doubt—if employees feel they can't trust the message, it won't matter how well-crafted it is. Ideally, you'd show them data, some form of concrete evidence to demonstrate you mean what you say, but with regulatory concerns, the need for secrecy, and sequenced decision-making, it can feel like the very nature of M&A is preventing you from being transparent.

But there is a way to concretize your narrative, despite these restrictions: promote the process. While you can't come out and say how you'll run the combined companies, you can reveal how you and your team will reach the decisions along the way. This could be, for example, the planning process the company will follow during the integration period, or the decision-making process regarding who should be appointed to major positions in the new entity. By speaking transparently at the procedural level, you engender trust by pulling the curtain back for your stakeholders, even if they might not find the eventual outcome favorable.

For P&G's deal with Gillette, this approach played a vital role in helping employees from both organizations digest the decision to "field the best team."[32] In the week before Gillette announced its first senior management appointments, IMO leadership released a memo stating how much they expected to reduce the workforce by, specifying that cuts would likely be made in both overlapping and non-overlapping areas, and assuring employees that they would receive appropriate notice and support if they lost their jobs.

The goal behind this memo was to provide what pre-eminent sociologist and Harvard business professor Rosabeth Moss Kanter termed "certainty of process," a productive way to help people cope with uncertainty by "provid[ing] clarity about when [and how] information will be provided."[33] Moheet Nagrath, then-Vice President of HR for P&G and a key Integration Leader, explained why they chose this route: "[I]f you can't tell people what the result or the outcome is, explain the process. That will help relieve the anxiety and then when the outcome comes, it comes… Even though [employees] don't know whether [they'll] have a job or not, [they] at least know what the process is to get there."

Promoting the process also helps to prevent against unintended signals and misunderstandings. Imagine, for instance, that you're in those critical first days after the announcement. Mindful of easing your people's anxieties and building momentum, you prepare an exciting update: your trusted CFO will serve as head of the IMO. With this announcement, you mean to provide clarity and clear leadership, but some might read into it further than you intend. Elevating the CFO must mean the deal will focus more on the numbers than the operators, they'll say.

You may find that M&A's disruptive reputation will push many, especially those who don't yet know you, to weigh what you're saying just as much as what it seems you're not. But this kind of speculation becomes much harder if you promote the process around these leadership decisions (e.g., highlighting the relevant qualities the CFO brings to the table, connecting those qualities to further appointments, sketching the expected timeline for those decisions) and tie it all back to your core message (how this decision and the coming appointments help the organization achieve a successful outcome according to your deal rationale).

Committing to promoting the process fundamentally primes the organization to work toward integration success in ways that the typical command structure cannot. Very soon after Rio Tinto and Alcan merged, a glaring problem emerged: neither company's people could contact the other's through internal systems. By all indications, it was a huge systems issue in the making, one that could set the integration back for who knew how long. But rather than trumpeting an "all fine" message and working away at a systems integration in frantic silence, the IMO decided to bring together the corporate staff's administrative assistants for a lunch to explain the problem.

In the days that followed, these support staff became grassroots champions for the process, not only alerting those in their spheres about the ongoing email problem but also developing alternative methods of communication that served as lifelines until the main system could be brought online. By bringing these administrators into the fold, the IMO was able to circumvent a significant obstacle while building vital buy-in through the newly combined organization to the processes critical for integration success.

CALIBRATING THE CADENCE

Let me address this chapter's elephant in the room: How often should you and your team communicate through the integration? It's one thing to craft a message, tailor it to different stakeholders, and promote the process underlying integration decision-making, but knowing when to send those messages out constitutes a distinct challenge of its own. And the research does show—empirically—that both the timing and content of communication through a deal's lifetime impact employee commitment to the organization.[34] So what timing produces the most positive impact?

Like so many other integration elements, the specific timing is dependent on your deal, though the cadence should generally track across key milestones. At McKinsey, my colleagues and I would think of these milestones across different phases, spanning due diligence through integration implementation to the eventual stabilization winding down the effort. Figure 5.3, on the next page, represents one way to visualize this milestone-based cadence, with both the announcement and Day One unsurprisingly standing out as high points. In the period of steady increase that connects them, internal communications comprise the majority, while external communications ramp up significantly as Day One approaches. Implementation, meanwhile, maintains a relatively consistent tempo built around specific milestones and updates, like hitting targets or announcing major changes.

This is just one example that speaks to a broader truth: people simply need reinforcement for a message to stick. This is especially true in

Figure 5.3   Example communication cadence.

SOURCE: Adapted from Oliver Engert, Becky Kaetzler, Kameron Kordestani, and Anish Koshy, "Communications in Mergers: The Glue That Holds Everything Together," McKinsey & Company, January 30, 2019, https://www.mckinsey.com/capabilities/people-and-organizational-performance/our-insights/communications-in-mergers-the-glue-that-holds-everything-together (accessed January 9, 2025).

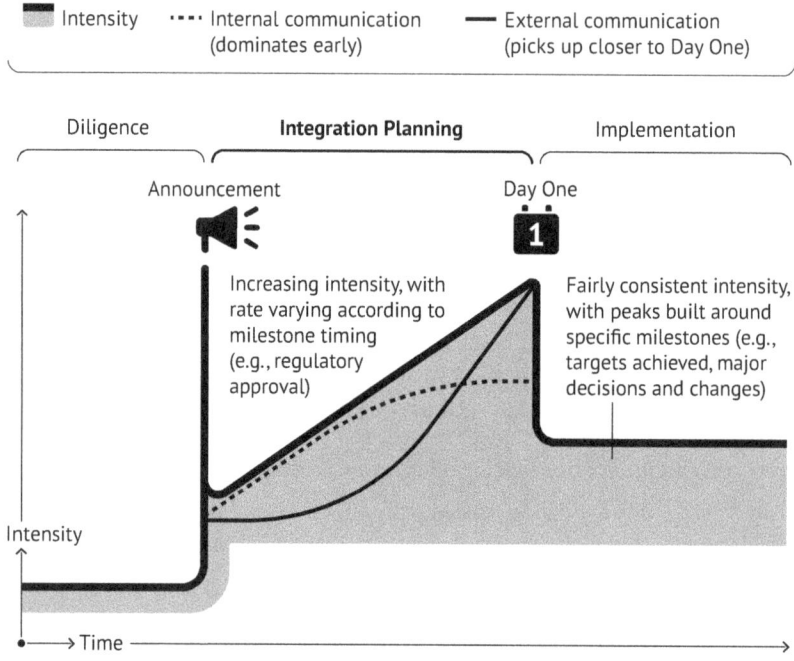

the integration context, when subordinates can often feel that they haven't been informed "properly" by their superiors, despite their superiors feeling convinced that they've communicated the right amount (a vexing perception gap).[35] Providing frequent touchpoints thus helps to keep your narrative relevant and fresh in the minds of your audience—and adds an attention-holding sense of progress and development that maintains buy-in. And, since the quality of those touchpoints also matters,[36] it does so more effectively and efficiently than just blasting out a constant stream of information, which is hardly a good use of what valuable, limited time you have.

As a result, as you go through the exercise of identifying your stakeholders and tailoring your message to them, take the opportunity to also consider the milestones that will be relevant to them. If you're planning on consolidating a few Midwest offices into your existing Chicago center, for example, those milestones could include determining the timelines for decision-making and implementation, announcing the decision itself, developing packages based on what they want to do, and so on. And with each message, you want to ensure that you promote the process behind your decisions, highlight the big-picture reason for this change, and acknowledge what it will mean for them. By connecting both the content and timing of your messages to their bespoke role in the deal, you treat them as valued partners—one you can lead and guide as you feel your way through integration.

STAYING ON MESSAGE WHILE STAYING GROUNDED

If all this seems overwhelming, allow me to share some closing words of calm. Remember that this is a shared responsibility. While the CEO is responsible for addressing the analyst community as well as the major political ones, other leaders should also contribute to the communication process. The IMO, for one, plays a critical role in developing and executing the communications strategy based on the core message you craft. And Integration Team leaders also share significant communication responsibilities, making sure everyone in their sphere is plugged into the rationale for the deal and how that is informing the processes they're following. Don't forget that internal and external communication staff are also there to support at the granular level of execution—writing press releases, speeches, digital messaging, and so on.

In fact, these players are indispensable for more than just getting the word out—it's their participation and buy-in that will allow your vision to solidify into a narrative that sticks. They are your storytellers. Everything they do should exude the narrative. If you can accomplish this, your story will quickly become truth, and your organization will become aligned toward the goal you had set out.

ACTION ITEMS IN REVIEW

- **Formulate your deal narrative based on your rationale**—and tailor each message according to your target stakeholder's bespoke interest in the deal.
- **Empower all Integration Teams to parrot the same message**—all 300 people working under the CEO on the integration should reinforce the deal narrative.
- **Over time, you can increasingly share the reasons for the deal**—but leadership must understand the rationale the whole way through.
- **Talk about process, rather than results**—especially while under regulatory review.

CHAPTER SIX

DAY ONE: MUST DOS AND NONESSENTIALS

You used to hear it ringing through the halls. A droning, excited buzz—relief, anticipation, a little exhaustion. Sometimes punctuated by festive clinks and pops, it seemed to say, "To a job well done!" But there was always something off about it. Because while the deal may have been announced to great fanfare, the real work hadn't even begun, not really. It was still a long road to Day One.

In the wake of the frenzied build up to Announcement Day, Day One often looms like a deadline you wish wouldn't come yet can't wait to get behind you. As you await the nod from regulators and get to work planning for the coming integration, you come face to face with the inescapable realization of all there is to do ahead of the fast-approaching deadline of legal close. By the time it rolls around, the afterglow has dissipated, and in its place, the weight of expectation has set in.

Those with limited deal experience can turn Day One into something massive. Suddenly, in their minds, Day One becomes the determinant of success for the integration—and thus the entire deal—a day that must go off without a hitch. If they can just nail Day One, they convince themselves, everything else will fall into place. But with so much riding on that single day, the pressure mounts to ready as much as possible in order to meet the moment. From new branding to unified systems and any number of organizational and operational initiatives to mark this moment of union, the agenda grows longer and longer, the scale of the to-dos, increasingly untenable.

But the truth is that integration doesn't succeed because of what happens on Day One. Rather, it succeeds because the right things happen *by* Day One, which in turn allows leaders to execute the rest that follows with discipline, sequencing, and staying power. My motto for you is thus quite simple: **Don't make Day One bigger than it needs to be.**

This chapter is about how to approach Day One with realism, clarity, and restraint. We'll focus on what *must* be in place—leadership decisions, business continuity, and risk mitigation—and what can wait, even if it's tempting to do it all at once. Done right, Day One won't be a dramatic debut, but a confident step onto new ground with your eyes wide open and your priorities clear.

PRELUDE: DEFINING "DAY ONE"

First, I want to ensure we're clear on what Day One actually refers to. Particularly among those new to a deal environment and folks in the press, I've noticed a conflation with the Announcement Day, which likely stems from the way many companies formulate their announcements. Let me show you what I mean:

> [Udemy] today announced the acquisition of Lummi... Now part of Udemy's Innovation Studio, the Lummi team will play a key role in...[1]
>
> Kering Eyewear announces the acquisition of Italian manufacturer Lenti, adding further capacity to its industrial footprint... The acquisition of

Lenti is another milestone in the ongoing industrial development strategy of Kering Eyewear...[2]

[Aya Healthcare] today announced the acquisition of Locum's Nest... This combination unites two leading providers in their respective countries...[3]

The language here gives a strong sense of finality: with these announcements, the deals are done and the companies, one. But despite this impression, it will be months before these players are given the necessary regulatory go-ahead for their deals to go through. Even private deals take time for legal reviews and negotiations. Day One for the yet-to-be-combined companies, in other words, is still a way off. This is not splitting semantic hairs: the fuzziness here can easily lead to unrealistic expectations around the integration timeframe and the priority list therein.

A second misconception leans too heavily into its symbolism as a day of new beginnings, the start of a new era. After all, history tempts us with turning points. As kids, we're taught to find clarity in big dates: 1776, 1945, 1989. In business, it's tempting to think of a deal in the same way, with a "before" and "after," pre- and post-merger. But historians urge us to see continuities across major moments of change. The Great Crash of 1929 was less the sudden collapse of the Roaring Twenties than the result of years of speculative bubbles, severe income inequality, agricultural depression, and other issues that continued to coalesce into the Great Depression of the following decade. And we've come to see how the fall of the Soviet Union hardly settled the tensions that defined the Cold War era. In much the same way, seasoned dealmakers know that Day One is less a clean break than it is the first step of a slow and careful grafting.

So, enough with misconceptions—when I say Day One, I'm talking about the day when the buyer takes formal, legal ownership of the assets and liabilities of the target company. It comes only after regulatory approval, when all closing conditions have been met. More than symbolic, it's a day of substantial legal and pragmatic significance: it's the day you *own* (exchange $$$), the day integration becomes real, and the day you begin the hard work of bringing two companies under a single roof—not just in brand, but in operations, governance, and accountability. It's a day you have to specifically prepare for.

The nature of that preparation becomes clearer by thinking of Day One as a bridge. When a deal closes, both companies still function as they did the day before. Though now under a shared roof, their systems, habits, and responsibilities largely remain intact. That's, of course, what makes integration so arduous and time-consuming, and why leaders who treat Day One as a moment of transformation, rather than the launch of a multiyear transformation *process*, set themselves up for disappointment (or worse). As a result, preparing for Day One constitutes the ultimate in prioritization exercises,[4] one which requires getting down to the elements that will most fundamentally create or could most effectively destroy value for the merged businesses. By having those items ready to cross the bridge by Day One's arrival, your organization will be better equipped for the remainder of the journey that lies on the other side.

TAKING THE HELM: LEADERSHIP AND THE PERSONNEL CASCADE

Day One first and foremost requires clarity at the top. Amid so much uncertainty, this moment is an opportunity to signal confidence and control by announcing the leaders who will steer the combined company through the next phase of its existence. Much like in Chapter Five, this signaling will impart a sense of stability that both your employees and the markets will appreciate. But even more valuable is the real organizational stability that comes from readying critical leadership decisions in advance of Day One.

This is more than calming nerves. It's about enabling cascading decisions throughout the organization toward a unified mandate—or, as colleagues and I urged nearly 20 years ago, "striv[ing] to *complete* the integration at the apex of the company *before* the close."[5]

By Day One, you should prioritize these key leadership actions:

- Resolving the CEO structure (including the handling of the acquired CEO)
- Finalizing the board composition
- Selecting and aligning at least Tier 1 and Tier 2 leadership to support the ongoing operations of the combined company

Your organization's readiness begins here. That's why the CEO and board arrangements are typically negotiated ahead of the deal: they're the seeds of integration planning planted during due diligence and grounded in the deal rationale. Deliberations for the remaining top management positions also tend to begin as early as due diligence, though they can't be finalized and announced until regulatory approval. Even when the selection process is sensitive, as with a "merger of equals"-type deal, any delays past Day One will stall the cascade that builds the new organization, undermining not only how quickly and effectively your organization can fully integrate, but also confidence in the emerging organization before integration truly gets underway. These aren't symbolic choices, but operational necessities for both the integration and the base business to attain success.

Let's start with the acquired CEO: in short, trying to appease a retiring executive with an ill-defined role often backfires. There are certainly circumstances when it makes strategic sense to keep them, but only if their continued presence will help to realize the vision for the new organization. I saw the consequences of such top-level misalignment some years ago when I was asked to help with an ongoing integration that had taken a turn for the worse. Things just weren't gelling, and persistent pre-existing differences kept getting in the way. This genuinely surprised many on the new leadership team, who felt there had been goodwill on both sides to come together. The CEO had even decided to keep on his counterpart from the acquired company as a gesture to his new employees. Given how well the two had gotten along and how beloved the acquired CEO was (not to mention close to retirement), the new senior executive thought it wouldn't hurt to have him on the Steering Committee during integration planning.

It turns out, however, that the acquired CEO had been working hard behind the scenes to advocate for his people every chance he could. His intent wasn't malicious, but he lacked alignment with the new vision for the organization, and his advocacy ultimately disrupted leadership selection ahead of Day One while simultaneously increasing feelings of rivalry within the top layers. By allowing him to continue exerting influence informally—lobbying for allies, second-guessing appointments, even undermining decisions—the decision introduced instability precisely when clarity was needed.

Similarly, in determining the composition of your board, your decision should also reflect the future more than the past. In a standard deal, the balance of power often dictates the numbers: as part of the financial agreement, the two sides might arrange for proportional representation somewhere between an even split (a theoretical true merger of equals) and unilateral control (a true takeover).[6] But board composition runs deeper than numerical representation. Just as members bring different talents, connections, and opportunities to the table, so too do they bring their own perspectives on the direction the company should go. While few deals will go the way of HP–Compaq, where the board took center stage in a protracted fight for the very "heart and soul" of the company,[7] members can become obstacles if they're not aligned with new management's vision. Even when the numbers are pre-negotiated, the priority must be setting a governance framework that supports the new strategy right from Day One.

The Personnel Cascade: Selecting and Aligning Senior Leaders on Down

You'll also need enough operational leaders in place to ensure your newly merged organization is aligned around clear goals from the start of integration. This, of course, starts with the C-suite, for which alignment is paramount. As Doug Parker shared:

> With the [troubled] Continental–United deal, they agreed that the leadership team would be equally balanced between the two organizations. The American side wanted us to head down a similar path, but we had seen how poorly that worked. We finally broke through when I agreed that Tom Horton [then American Airlines CEO and Chairman] would remain as chairman of the board. But I was going to be the CEO, and my perspective was that, as CEO, I should have the team that I work with best, and that was my team from US. We sprinkled in a few from American, but only because they fit in perfectly with the culture.[8]

But these leadership decisions aren't limited to just your C-suite. Rather, by Day One, you should have selected your senior leadership (often referred to as Tier 1), and they should have selected the next level of leaders below them (Tier 2), much like a cascade flowing down through the ranks. In total, this often translates to about 60 people ready to lead the merged company right from legal close. Figure 6.1, on the next page, represents a simplified version of this cascade.

Tier 3 can get trickier. For this subsequent tier (reaching roughly 250 in total), some decide to wait until after Day One in order to hold staff in place for base business protection. I prefer to err on the side of decisiveness and advise that they also be decided ahead of Day One, as is feasible. The leaders at this level are sure to be approached by headhunters or even competitors,[9] which means that waiting too long, especially past Day One,

Figure 6.1   The Personnel Cascade.

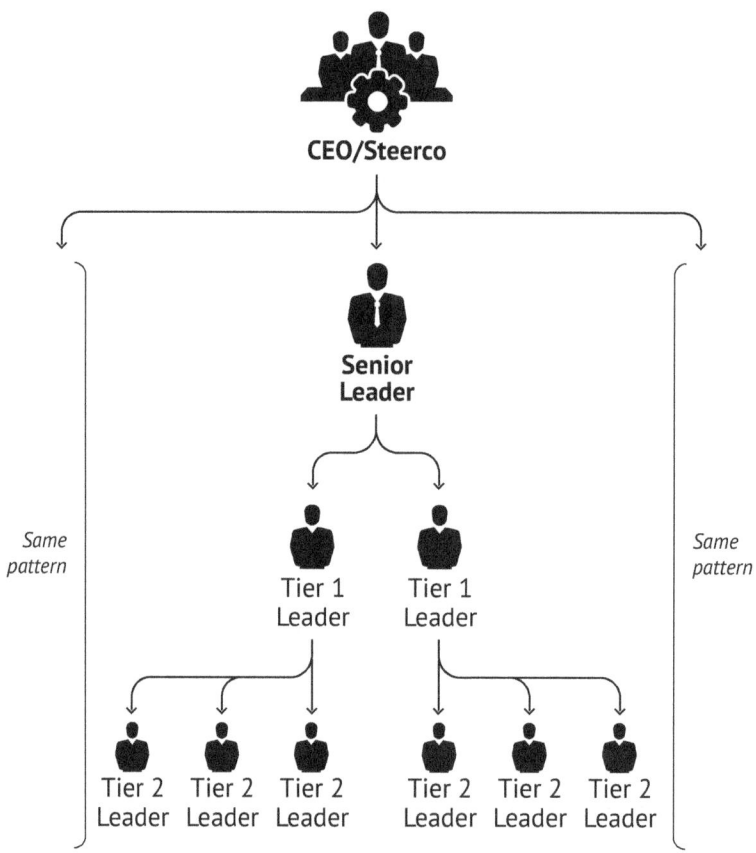

risks losing valuable talent that your Newco would benefit from. (Though, if necessary, the targeted communication strategies from Chapter Five can help mitigate some of this risk.)

The flipside, of course, is that you must also decide which leaders will be leaving. Many acquiring CEOs already know who will populate their C-suite, or in the case of explicit mergers, at least know which positions are non-negotiable. Here, departing C-level executives are often notified discretely ahead of close to ease the transition process. Tier 2 leaders like Senior Vice Presidents, meanwhile, are typically notified close to or on Day One to maintain business continuity. Tier 3 could also come around the same time, or otherwise shortly after Day One, depending on the timing of their selection, followed by the remaining tiers down the cascade. In all cases, the acquirer treats the cost of the Tier 1 "golden parachutes" provisions and other severance packages against anticipated headcount synergies as a cost of doing business.

It's critical to make these decisions quickly, though that's easier said than done. Even under normal circumstances, ensuring strategic alignment often gets harder the further down the ranks you go.[10] Considering the added hurdle of selecting among candidates who are not only relatively unknown to, but also potentially skeptical of or even antagonistic toward, acquiring leadership, it's understandable that some like to take extra time to get to know the other side before making their selections. In some cases, you (or those below you) will know specifically who you want where, but the closer you get to a "true" merger, it may make more sense to flesh out the roles you need first, then make your selections from a joint pool accordingly.[11]

Regardless of how you go about it, delaying these decisions only works counter to deal success by slowing your organization's ability to act and increasing the anxiety that comes from ambiguity. That's why it's all the more useful to prioritize these leadership decisions among a focused pre-Day One agenda in order to shore up confidence and increase alignment from the top down.

BUSINESS ESSENTIALS: CONTINUITY AND PREVENTION

While leadership decisions set the tone, business continuity and liability protection are the "make or break" items that keep the company—now inclusive of all your acquired assets—functioning. Here, continuity means protecting the commercial engine: orders, billings, payables, receivables, and service. Liability, meanwhile, translates to managing risk. When you take ownership of another company's assets, you also inherit its problems, meaning that safety protocols, legal exposure, and operational standards all transfer to you. If the worst happens and a plant explodes or a tanker runs aground, it's your legal responsibility and your name in the headlines.

In short, by the dawn of Day One, you must ensure that:

- Customers can be served
- Vendors can be paid
- Employees can be paid
- Legal and regulatory obligations are met
- Safety and compliance are not compromised

This isn't glamorous work, but it is essential. To harken back to Chapter One, this work to maintain the base business correlates strongly with deal success, as McKinsey has shown: though many deals suffer from a drop in base revenue during the first year, over 70% of successful deals were able to avoid this "year-one dip" by proactively protecting the base business.[12] In other words, by stabilizing operations immediately, your deal has a significantly higher chance to deliver expected value. And when compared to other items on the long integration to-do list, it's easy to see why continuity and liability should be top priority: if your combined company can't run, you don't have time to worry about logos or email addresses.

This became a critical point of discussion as Chevron and Texaco planned for their merger. It was the eve of close, and several key executives were fixated on branding. What should the new logo look like, and what's the ideal way to handle the rollout? But with Day One right around the corner, it took a hard conversation to remind Chevron leadership about more pressing priorities: "If a Texaco tanker spills tomorrow, it's yours." And while, thankfully, that scenario didn't come to pass, the company did inherit other environmental liabilities that would eventually surface, such as a class action lawsuit that has continued to play out to the tune of nearly $10 billion.[13]

Or take the case of Boston Scientific's thorny acquisition of Guidant, a medical device company. Despite initially negotiating an acquisition by Johnson & Johnson, Guidant's surprise recall of its defibrillators in June 2005 pushed Johnson & Johnson to reconsider, which allowed Boston Scientific to swoop in with a higher bid (a move that eventually resulted in a $600 million settlement to Johnson & Johnson for impropriety).[14] But as it came to learn, it inherited more than just promising technology in the deal: after the Food and Drug Administration found that Guidant had knowingly hidden the faults behind the recalls, it was Boston Scientific that was on the hook for the $296 million penalty.[15]

The bottom line for Day One is to focus on what can shut you down or create irreversible harm. That's why American Airlines and US Airways, despite the (literally) dozens of priorities the integration planners identified, always put passenger safety first. Both sides realized that business continuity and liability prevention were just two sides of the same coin. Whether from a systems error or a hardware malfunction, it wouldn't matter—their very reason for existing was on the line. Everything else could wait.

THE THINGS THAT CAN WAIT

Integration is long, but Day One is short. And while the list of to-dos might only seem to grow the closer you get to implementation, your IMO can only handle so much at once. Not everything can or should be a Day-One priority, even if they're important. In fact, the reality is that virtually every deal will require the two sides to run some systems in parallel for months (or longer)—so best to plan accordingly.

These are the things that are often desired but rarely on the critical path:

- **Branding and signage.** It's tempting to show off a new identity right away, but rebranding every asset, office, and document on Day One is a logistical fantasy that's better done in phases.
- **Physical consolidation.** Moving headquarters or combining manufacturing sites takes time and planning. These are high-stakes, emotional decisions that you can't afford to rush.
- **Systems and IT.** Merging tech platforms can take *years*. Whether it's payroll or enterprise software, most integrations require parallel systems for a long while (often longer than you first expect). That's normal.
- **Communications (email).** Setting aside the effort it can take to have new email addresses and merged directories ready and bug-free, people often feel attached to their domains.[16] You can make these changes more effectively as part of cultural integration.
- **Procurement.** It's a key synergy lever (often the biggest synergy source for Year One), but alignment with suppliers often lags Day One. Procurement is a perfect case to apply advice from legendary UCLA basketball coach John Wooden: "Be quick, but don't hurry."[17] Set expectations and move quickly post-close, but don't try to unify everything on Day One.

In short, in determining your priorities, be deliberate, not theatrical. Don't let pressure for symbolism override operational logic. If it isn't critical for running the business or preventing harm, it can wait.

KEEPING DAY ONE REALISTIC

All in all, aim to keep your agenda and expectations for Day One realistic. That starts with aligning your priorities around the bare minimum of the most essential, the "make or breaks" of leadership, continuity, and risk.

Figure 6.2   Planning for Day One.

Planning for Day One			
	Must Do		Nonessential
Address Leadership	CEO Alignment		Branding and Signage
	Board Alignment		Physical Consolidation
	Personnel Cascade		Systems and IT
Ensure Business Continuity			Communication/email
Anticipate Liability + Safety Issues			Procurement

While these considerations (summarized in Figure 6.2) aren't exhaustive, they are the kinds of decisions I had to discuss with CEOs on deal after deal with the most urgency, the throughline preparations connecting many Day Ones. If integration planning and execution are extreme exercises in prioritization, then prepping for Day One is the pinnacle: as important as everything else is, the rest is better left staged and sequenced.

This realistic approach is just as much for your organization overall as it is for your team. Your IMO will be stretched thin right from the start, so by keeping the scope of Day One priorities manageable, you're also allowing them to conserve the energy and attention they'll need for the long haul. For however much integration feels like a sprint, it requires a marathon mentality to make it through to the end in one piece, because after Day One comes Day Two, Day Three … and often Day 800. By taking that long-term perspective, it's easier to realize that integration success isn't born on Day One—it's launched by it.

At the same time, expect bumps and challenges. Things can go off in unexpected ways under far less complex circumstances than wiring two companies together, even with rigorous prioritization and planning. Remember that, as critical as it is to ensure the essentials are met, integration success will depend less on what happens in the first 24 hours than on the next 24 months. As a result, realize the value in doing less, better, to ensure your first step is sure-footed.

ACTION ITEMS IN REVIEW

- **Finalize leadership for the new organization**—address the CEO and board balance, and kick off the Personnel Cascade through at least Tier 1 and Tier 2 positions ahead of Day One.
- **Ensure continuity of the core operation "makes"**—like billing and payroll.
- **Anticipate early and thoroughly address potential "breaks"**—like liability and safety risks.
- **Defer longer-term and less urgent decisions until after Day One**—like branding, IT integration, and real estate decisions (unless mission critical).

PART III

IMPLEMENT: RUNNING THE INTEGRATION AND BEYOND

CHAPTER SEVEN

INITIAL INTEGRATION: THE PARALLEL PROCESS IN THE TRANSITION TO IMPLEMENTATION

D ay One comes and, in an instant, the implementation has begun. With the two entities now legally combined, months of planning can finally translate to concrete action. But in the excitement to implement, there's also an irony: from the action needed to bring both sides together, will spring the very things that most threaten the ultimate success of the integration. Employee anxieties around expected cuts and changes, loss of focus on customer needs amid internal initiatives, milestones missed from slowing momentum or leaders' discontent with their new roles and assigned integration plans—every action can produce its own countervailing reaction.

Thankfully, your integration effort already has a system in place to address these challenges: the Parallel Process. What allowed your planning effort to proceed without extra baggage from the base business is now poised to guide business units toward the goals set out for them. Some changes will, of course, be necessary in the transition as leaders take on new responsibilities and the organization works toward new priorities. But the principle of separation, now transformed into added oversight, remains the tracks upon which the effort moves along.

This short chapter is all about the immediate changes that happen in the initial stages of the implementation. It starts by outlining the evolving form of the Parallel Process, in particular how the IMO transitions into a coordinative and tracking role. Then, a quick note on a frequent debate around the pace of integration at the outset of implementation. Lastly, the discussion turns to some of the things to look out for that could signal an integration gone awry. Overall, this conversation focuses on the procedural elements of early implementation, ahead of the focus on culture and personnel issues in Chapter Eight.

MONITORING AND REPORTING: THE NEXT PHASE OF THE PARALLEL PROCESS

To this point in the integration, the efficacy of your organization's planning effort has depended on the Parallel Process. In the months and weeks prior to Day One, Steerco has empowered the IMO and the Integration Teams to work autonomously and independent of the base business. This dual system has helped to keep the planning effort tightly focused on the aspirations for the deal, as free as possible from tangential/special interests, and efficient, while fundamentally acknowledging the higher degree of uncertainty with which the integration planners have had to contend.

Even once planning has concluded, the Parallel Process continues to play a vital role in the integration effort, starting with the functional leaders. It starts with a commitment made to the CEO/C-suite, as they accept their role with the future organization: during the selection process, it's important that top management require all new business unit and functional leaders to accept the plan assigned by the IMO and work toward its implementation as a condition of their appointment.

Some leaders may be reluctant to do this, whether because they'd prefer to adopt a different path, because they want a plan that's wholly theirs, or even because they were never in full agreement with it while it was being formulated. But as CEO Dennis Picard repeatedly drove home as he oversaw Raytheon's acquisition of Hughes, it didn't matter what they thought of the plans. Even if they end up being a starting point that needs to be revised later down the line, by accepting the job, the leaders accepted the plans.

The flipside of this commitment involves a shift in the responsibilities of the IMO. Now that the plans have been drawn up and given to the business leaders to implement, the IMO concludes its strategic role and focuses on project management and monitoring. In effect, the IMO now functions to hold the various parts of the merged business accountable, and in so doing, they enforce a separate tracking process (a separate set of books) focused on the adoption of the integration goals.

The IMO in Transition: New Responsibilities

Switching into implementation, the IMO must now ensure that the plans are as clear as possible, understood (to the extent they can be), and implemented as designed, to ensure the whole mosaic of efforts is launched successfully. Regardless of any fatigue that may have set in, the team must maintain momentum by continuing their tracking process with all business units/functional areas assigned an integration plan. This tracking includes a regular cadence of meetings that facilitate transparency and coordination across units, as well as dedicated progress reporting to the IMO beyond the existing reporting to their functional bosses. The IMO then aggregates this data and reports to the CEO/C-suite on the ongoing progress of the integration.

In this shift to tracking and coordinating, the team may be reduced in size and time commitment. This partially reflects the (relative) downshift in intensity of their work, compared to spearheading the planning effort. But more importantly, it's a practical necessity given the nature of the average IMO member, who was likely selected in light of their leadership potential in the combined organization. Think back to Robert Isom, Doug Parker's righthand man, in Chapter Two: as the post-merger American Airlines came into being, he had to juggle his remaining duties as IMO Leader with his new responsibilities as COO simultaneously.

Teams may differ in their preferred approach, though it helps to come in with a clear plan. They'll benefit from providing a structure for themselves and for functional leaders to help with translating and tracking the plans they agreed to. It's also common for a less senior member of the IMO to step in to free up senior members (like a Robert Isom) for their other executive functions. Alternatively, for organizations with resources like a Transformation Office, dedicated staff may step in to shoulder more of the load. In any case, no matter how busy they may be, the IMO will stay engaged to keep the integration moving forward on the right track and ensure the transition from planning to implementation.

As for how long they'll need to keep up this work, the answer once again varies from deal to deal. Typically, the tracking cadence runs through at least the first three months of the integration's implementation, though as Chapter Nine will address, it often goes longer. This usually comes down to the complexity of the integration: a takeover, for example, typically requires less change on the acquirer's end (e.g., same management team, fewer cultural questions, limited systems work), which in turn means there are fewer things for the IMO to track over a (potentially) shorter period. But as is so often the case, the "right" amount of time is less about a predetermined, hard-set timeframe and instead more concerned with ensuring business units take full ownership of their integration plans and demonstrate clear progress toward their implementation.

A NOTE ON SPEED AND THE FIRST 100 DAYS

"The first 100 days post-merger are crucial for long-term success."[1]
"The first 100 days post-M&A are pivotal…"[2]
"The first 100 days of a merger have a disproportionately high impact on the overall success of an integration… Thus, having a plan for the first 100 days in place decides over the success of a post-merger integration."[3]

The "first 100 days" paradigm, a mainstay of integration discourse for decades, holds that the first 100 days post-close mark the critical period for integration success. As a result, purists may say, leaders need to work fast. As far back as 2004, scholars like Duncan Angwin were already making the case that this paradigm is more a matter of convenience than a hard and fast truth, and have cautioned that integrating quickly for its own sake can produce unforced errors.[4] Other scholars have also echoed this perspective, highlighting the economic costs of rushing and the increased anxiety it can produce among employees, while advocating for a deliberate approach to mitigate feelings of uncertainty and build trust within the combined organization.[5] All the same, outside of academia, the 100-day mark remains influential.

When it comes to the pace of integration, *deliberate* is an appropriate word: rather than optimizing for a fast or slow approach, integration planners should calibrate their pace in specific areas according to the needs and goals of the deal. In fact, the pace of integration may need to vary not only according to, for example, business unit, but also over different stages of the implementation. For example, from an organization-wide perspective, achieving quick wins is vital to building momentum, and the outside world (particularly investors) will often judge the success or failure of a merger by the progress made within 12–18 months of close. But achieving complete systems integration may take more time and benefit from a steady rollout to avoid costly mistakes.

In fact, for some areas, it's less about pace than identifying and acting on key milestones. Under the large umbrella of cultural integration, for example, there's proven value in addressing employee anxieties and generating buy-in early in the integration,[6] but the "end state" of cultural integration success can sometimes take multiple years to achieve. Particularly for transformation efforts (which cultural integration often is), the appropriate pace may vary over successive "waves" of the effort, as a group from McKinsey has argued, sometimes in ways counter to expectation: "Despite a common perception that the intensity of an integration decreases over time, in some cases," particularly when the integration effort entails transformation initiatives, "more or different resources are needed in successive phases than in initial ones" to keep energy high and take advantage of emergent opportunities.[7]

The mindset here adheres to the piece of Coach Wooden's philosophy I referenced in Chapter Six: "Be quick, but don't hurry." Adapted from an adage popular among the Ancient Greeks and Romans, Wooden's wisdom urges against haste in decision-making and rashness in implementation, instead encouraging decisive but levelheaded action. Because, as the coach often used to ask of his students, "If you don't have time to do it right, when will you have time to do it over?"[8]

SIGNS OF AN INTEGRATION GOING WRONG

Once an organization starts implementing the changes it planned for, it's critical to stay alert for signs of things going wrong. An integration effort is bound to face trouble spots by the very nature of bringing together different groups of people with different ways of operating, and sometimes conditions change midway through the process, forcing plans to change. But too many trouble spots can signal the poor health of not just the integration effort, but the overall merging organization as well.

Some signals easily attract focus. External 'signposts like poor market reactions or supply disruptions are particularly visible. Moreover, in their tracking role, the IMO will be particularly attuned to units missing milestones, failing to achieve targets, or their leaders otherwise feeling disconnected from or consistently hostile to the expectations on them.

But for other signs, it will take attentiveness from leaders outside the IMO to the kinds of internal and external stakeholders highlighted in Chapter Five. Internally, are key managers and employees expressing dissatisfaction, or even leaving? If they're expressing dissatisfaction, is it due to procedural aspects (e.g., feelings of uncertainty), intended results of the integration (e.g., de-prioritization of an element of the business), or potential missteps (e.g., insufficient frequency or quality of communication, disconnect between stated goals and leaders' actions/behaviors)? What about customers and external partners? Are they continuing to be served, or at the very least communicated to clearly and consistently? Is the rate of churn increasing beyond usual levels? As basic as these questions are, they can easily go unnoticed without dedicated attention.

If warning signs start to appear, it's critical to react and adjust plans as needed. While Timothy Galpin and Mark Herndon provide a series of surveys and tools you can use to diagnose and address issues as part of a "merger repair" process,[9] the key is to err on the side of proactivity in raising potential issues to the IMO, who can step in to triage the situation and bring in the relevant functional leaders and executive oversight.

ACTION ITEMS IN REVIEW

- **Ensure functional leaders agree to accept the integration plans** given to them by the IMO as a condition of their appointment in the new organization.
- **Transition the IMO to the project management and coordination role** responsible for monitoring the progress of business units toward their assigned targets.
- **Establish a regular reporting cadence** between the functional leaders/ units and the IMO, in addition to regular business reporting.
- **Proactively look for problem signs** among internal and external stakeholders.

CHAPTER EIGHT

DOING IS BELIEVING: ORGANIZATIONAL CULTURE AND THE CHALLENGE OF CULTURAL INTEGRATION

How exactly are you supposed to integrate something as seemingly amorphous as culture? This question has dogged leaders almost since the genesis of M&A, and even with decades of studies and lessons learned that have meaningfully improved our general ability to secure value through integration, culture continues to cause immense problems. It's no surprise that leaders are constantly looking for the best way to go about cultural integration, but ironically, this search for a "best" tends to bring more disappointment than relief while creating more anxiety for planners, as they prepare for their arduous work ahead.

Rather than prescribing a way to run things, this chapter is designed to help you develop the approach best suited to your organization's needs. Let's first establish what culture is (and isn't) in the M&A context and talk a bit about why it continues to derail so many attempts at integration. Then, transitioning to the implementation level, I'll give a brief overview of the mistakes that most commonly lead cultural integration astray. Much of the remainder of the chapter is then dedicated to a phased approach to cultural integration meant to help you connect the culture change you want to your deal's rationale, while engaging the entirety of your integration effort in that change collectively. The chapter will lastly conclude with two cases, both cross-border deals, that speak to the value in connecting your approach to cultural integration to the deal rationale, even if the route there may seem unexpected.

CULTURAL (MIS)CONCEPTIONS: WHAT CULTURE IS AND ISN'T

Why is culture such a big issue in M&A? It's not from a lack of awareness, at least not anymore. In 2019, McKinsey found that 95% of polled executives recognized "cultural fit as critical to the success of integration."[1] And in a January 2023 survey of roughly 1,100 M&A leaders, the firm also found that 44% attributed integration failure to "lack of cultural fit" and "friction between acquiring and target companies."[2] Of course, failure isn't the only metric for difficulty: a Bain survey from the same year found that 80% of integrations began addressing cultural fit at the start of or even before due diligence, but 75% were nevertheless impacted enough by cultural issues to require serious intervention.[3] Clearly there's something systemic at work.

Firm understanding of culture (and specifically *organizational* culture) continues to elude many leaders in the M&A context. This isn't to fault them, since "culture" has been used and defined in so many hundreds of ways that the body of literature on it can best be described as "vast."[4] And, admittedly, general awareness in the corporate world has improved over the years: executives used to fixate on regional and national differences, as well as visible markers ("artifacts") like dress code and office layout,[5] and while those factors can still play a role,[6] leaders have largely gotten familiar with thinking past them. Still, they remain largely stuck at culture's importance in the abstract, rather than understanding how it works and how people engage with and shape it.

For M&A, organizational culture is all about mindsets and behaviors. It manifests in habits and workflows—the ways of doing and being that become second nature as people spend more time within the organization (as they become *acculturated*). Edgar Schein, who pioneered the modern study of organizational culture, called this deepest layer of culture our "underlying assumptions."[7] These assumptions are baked into how each of us works within our organizations. Author and business advisor Ram Charan, in analyzing how Home Depot redefined itself for exponential success in the early 2000s, recognized this connection, arguing that culture operates at the level of "social architecture," which he defined as "the collective ways in which people work together across an organization to support the business model."[8] A group from Boston Consulting Group summed it up well in defining culture as "an organization's values and characteristic set of behaviors, which collectively define *how things get done* in support of the organization's purpose and strategy" (emphasis mine).[9] Taken together, this view corroborates what industrial anthropologist John Shook gleaned over his years with Toyota: in order to change culture, you must change how people act before you can change how they think.[10]

Unlike practices, values leave room for interpretation—which can make the appearance of similarity dangerously deceptive even to teams with deep M&A experience. This includes Johnson & Johnson, as Aileen Stockburger, former Vice President of Worldwide Business Development, revealed in a

2018 interview: in one case, cursory assessments of the target's culture, colored by the well-intentioned desire to find overlap, gave the impression of similarity, when in reality, decision-making and leadership styles were so different that the target ended up floundering, and the majority of its leaders eventually departed.[11] I've seen situations like this, where leaders even celebrated their perceived similarity ahead of integration without digging into the substance behind their "shared" values. However, it turned out that for Company A, "collaboration" translated to formalized, regular, long-term, cross-functional engagement across the top few bands of leadership, while for Company B, it meant that employees turned to function-wide Slack channels for help. Though they used the same language, how they carried out their values differed drastically.

Case Study: P&G and Gillette[12]

P&G and Gillette came face-to-face with this dilemma. Their leaders expected things to go smoothly, given the many apparent similarities between the two companies: both were packaged goods organizations, both sold to retailers like Walmart, both had brand management structures that recruited the same types of people. Their value statements also seemed quite aligned, as both highlighted the importance of integrity, achievement, and their people. And, as an added bonus, CEO A.G. Lafley had just taken P&G through an intense but promising restructuring designed to make the storied company more innovative, collaborative, and flexible for global expansion—a process that Lafley believed had made P&G's culture much more compatible with Gillette's.

But were these apparent similarities enough? Before integration planning had concluded, leaders on both sides recognized the immensity of the task ahead of them. "The principles and the values were the same," admitted Ed Shirley, a legacy Gillette executive and future Group President for P&G North America. "The difference was in the culture."[13]

While both companies targeted separate demographics, the heart of the matter came down to a fundamental difference in decision-making. P&G was a conservative organization, steeped in tradition. It prided itself on its "promote-from-within" philosophy and reliance on internal social networks to push ideas through the organization in a way that fostered creativity and joint ownership at the cost of speed. P&G's way was "inquiry-based, consensus-driven, and iterative," which overall made its employees feel more like family than a team.[14]

Gillette, meanwhile, had moved away from the family mindset. Under CEO Jim Kilts, the first "outsider" to lead the company in over half a century,[15] the company had become much more agile to deal with global scale. Its organization had fewer structural layers and sought to drive a much more aggressive flow of information throughout the company, through "rigorous debate" and role clarity. Though this made Gillette feel "more top-down and autocratic," it also meant it could be more innovative and take more risks.[16]

Integrating these two global companies with their own distinct ways of operating proved considerably challenging. Communicating that the combined organization would take a "best of both" approach, while true to fact, sowed confusion and anxiety throughout both companies, as lifetime P&Gers expressed disbelief at the possibility of their replacement while Gillette staff questioned how much attention they'd really get as the acquired party. Realigning how members from either side needed to go about their work—which sometimes meant replacing P&G legacy practices with Gillette's—took time, patience, reinforcement, and proper incentives.

In the end, the integration did produce positive results and was fairly effective at overcoming the cultural divide: while only two top Gillette executives were left, within a year of the announcement, 60% of its top managers decided to stay with the company (beating the industry average by roughly 10%), while 90% of the "top talent" employees offered a position with the new organization chose to accept.[17] Nevertheless, it was a hard way to learn that culture is much more ingrained than principles and values—that dozens of points of outward similarity may not really translate to alignment in how things get done.

COMMON CULTURAL INTEGRATION MISTAKES

Let's dig into the most common problem signs for cultural integration:

- **Creating a "culture team" or relegating it to HR.** Drawing up a team to spearhead an effort is practically a business reflex, but culture is too systemic an issue for one single team to handle effectively. Relegating culture to the purview of one team elides the true complexity of the issue and easily results in surface-level tactics like putting slogans on walls and running trust-building exercises. In its systemic nature— how it permeates an organization—it resembles the equity initiatives of the early 2020s: many companies came to realize that just appointing a Chief Diversity Officer amounted to little more than a corporate pat on the back unless they dedicated enough resources to support a comprehensive effort.[18] As something that reaches every corner of the organization, culture must be owned by every team collectively.
- **Putting people in new roles and expecting cultural shifts to follow naturally.** This is wishful thinking. Even with new titles and responsibilities to foster fresh perspectives, people tend to fall back on what they're used to. Two years after HP bought Compaq, there were still people at the company who thought of themselves as a "Compaq guy" (or at least continued to act like one). It takes time, incentives, education—in other words, targeted and dedicated effort—for people to shift how they think about and behave at work, because whether consciously or not, they are also shifting how they think about *themselves*.

- **Failing to align incentives and rewards with desired cultural change.** Even with the right messaging and intentions, a merger won't change behaviors if people are promoted based on revenue alone. Instead, integration leadership must develop methods to incentivize, evaluate, and promote people that will align employees with their desired cultural end state. That's one way P&G and Gillette overcame lingering sentiments of "us versus them": rather than revenue, P&G created incentives tied to business momentum, fielding the best team from across both talent pools, project tracking, and more; maintained them for a few years past the end of integration; and extended them beyond the topmost levels.[19] Doug Parker and Robert Isom took a similar approach, ensuring to reward people for operational excellence while phasing out legacy American Airlines' incentives around marketing.

- **Espousing the mindset that "losers walk."** The thinking around acquisitions used to mimic American sports, where the acquirer was the "winner" and the target was the "loser," whose place it was to acquiesce. These days, though leaders are more mindful of avoiding this dynamic, even when the acquired side will have to make concessions, it can still creep its way in when tensions arise. Sometimes it can take on very literal significance when leaders from the acquired company are expected to relocate. Though much rarer now thanks to digital tools, some companies still feel strongly about this approach because they see it as key to cultural integration. Despite good intentions, Keurig Dr Pepper's integration struggled as legacy Pepper leaders tried to adjust from life in Texas to Massachusetts. Meanwhile, in their 2023 railroad merger, Canadian Pacific decided to make Kansas City Southern's headquarters its US headquarters over its existing Minneapolis office, a dual system that helped the two sides gel.

- **Ignoring the impact of virtual integration.** Though digital tools have made relocation much less necessary, remote/distanced integration can pose its own distinct challenges for employees. Acclimating to a new organization from the other side of a computer screen can be a particularly lonely experience that amplifies the feeling of difference among teams.[20] Creating opportunities to meet with new team members face-to-face—even if short of relocation—helps all parties establish mutual norms they're comfortable with, as well as the arrangements that work best individually and collectively.

- **Underestimating the extent of cultural differences.** When Unilever acquired Bestfoods in 2000, some analysts expected a simple cultural integration: after all, their North American headquarters were just a parking lot away! But appearances can be deceiving, and their two management styles were a world apart. Going in looking for differences is a much safer bet than being taken by surprise—especially when there's reason to expect similarity. Sometimes it even takes closely working together for differences to surface. Once integration work got underway for Canadian Pacific and Kansas City Southern, they began to notice how their approach to communications and proactivity differed in more concrete ways. All the same, even if one acted more as a "pitcher" and the other a "catcher," as one of their leaders described, they rightly recognized that it would still take both to construct a championship-caliber battery.

A PHASED APPROACH TO CULTURAL INTEGRATION

Now comes the hardest part: planning for, structuring, and implementing successful cultural integration. A perfect encapsulation of the difficulty of integration writ large, cultural integration has no one-size-fits-all solution. To confound things further, my career has taught me that cultural integration is much more an art than it is a science. Consequently, this phased approach is more about mindset than a rigid to-do list: its purpose is to help you think about culture in light of your deal rationale and sync your approach with other elements of your integration planning and implementation efforts.

Let's first revisit Kurt Lewin's model of organizational change from back in Chapter One. Stripped down to its simplest parts, his model instructs us to identify what we want to change, then devise ways to make that change, and finally implement continued action to ingrain that change.[21] From there, we'll need to add a few tailored elements. For example, since we have two different cultures coming together, we'll need to take stock of what we have (on both sides) before we can identify what we want to change. We'll also need to get a bit more specific about how to develop, promote, and implement change—for which we can look to John Kotter's foundational work on the subject.[22] In total, we're left with a series of phased steps that, despite some overlap, progress roughly sequentially, designed to help you assess what you have, identify what you want, and build toward your desired culture (see Figure 8.1, on the next page).

Phase 0: From Cultural Due Diligence and Self-Assessment to a Cultural Statement

If a successful merger starts with comprehensive due diligence, why shouldn't culture play a part? While you won't be able to get a full sense of your target's cultural reality, you may discover elements that you can begin planning for early—or even areas of clear disjuncture that dissuade you from pursuing the deal altogether. Like I advocated in Chapter Four, by broadening the scope of your due diligence beyond the financials by talking to suppliers, customers, analysts, and even former leaders, you can start developing a qualitative sense for the ways of doing and being that define your target.

Figure 8.1   A phased approach to cultural integration.

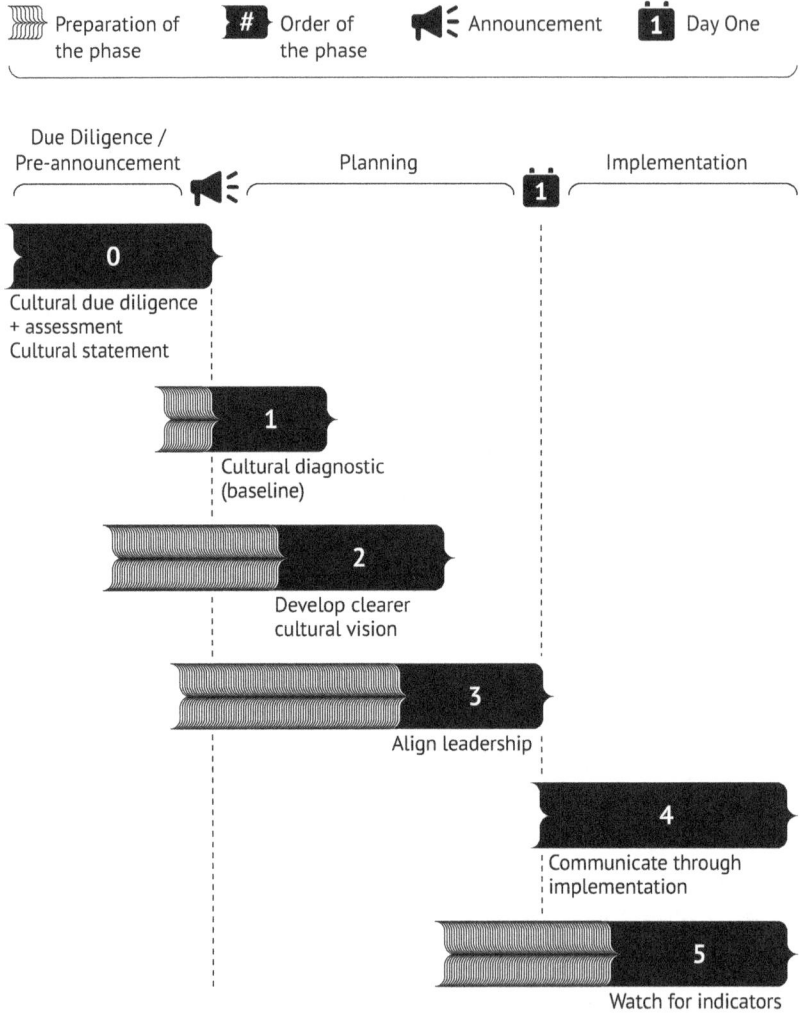

And in the same vein, it's also important to start assessing yourself. By taking the time to answer just a few questions, like "What makes us different?" "What's important around here?" "Which systems run this place?" and "What do we reward?" you can form, in clearer detail, the cultural basis from which your deal will work. This process could also help bring to the fore room for improvement or areas of internal misalignment during the subsequent stages of integration planning.

This self-assessment may also help you to sharpen your *cultural statement* for the deal. While only some deals will build their rationale explicitly around a culture change, every deal will draw a line in the sand regarding the cultural drivers of the new organization (even if it's "The acquired teams will have to adapt"). Recall how, in a deal built around scaling operations, Doug Parker never wavered in his conviction that the merged company prioritize on-time departures and arrivals and move away from the marketing and brand focus of the pre-merger American Airlines. Even as he and his senior leaders agreed to a range of compromises, this conviction ended up becoming the line in the sand—the deal's cultural statement—and it shaped the entirety of the work done for the integration. It also happened to answer each of the questions of the self-assessment above.

Phase 1: Conduct a Comprehensive Cultural Diagnostic (Cultural Baseline)

"If you don't measure it, it won't change." Just like with your other integration priorities, there's little hope of effectively changing culture without a clear sense of the pre-integration state. The process of measuring may itself look different (culture is far trickier to quantify), but it's a measuring process all the same. By asking the right questions in the right ways, your integration planners can develop, as they will across all other integration priorities, a detailed snapshot of how work gets done in *both* organizations prior to integration, that is, a cultural baseline.[23]

A quick example to illustrate the value of this cultural baseline: the merger between two leading pharmaceutical companies. On the surface,

Pharma A and Pharma B looked promisingly similar. More than just industry mates, they shared considerable overlap in their customer base, the locations of their respective offices and headquarters, and even elements of their founding stories. But those apparent similarities receded from view upon closer inspection. Pharma A was R&D-focused, and though it was interested in Pharma B primarily for its R&D assets, Pharma B's culture was driven more by sales. This meant that Pharma B tended to hire aggressive salespeople, while Pharma A preferred people who could build strong relationships with customers and use the knowledge they gained from those relationships to drive research. What many had taken for a strong, overlapping foundation had more gaps than anticipated.

By digging into how work got done in each company early in the process, the integration planners were able to uncover the extent of these fissures with enough time to adjust. Had they not done so, the divide would have emerged once implementation was already underway, and the odds of success would have become much slimmer. Instead of carefully rolling out a series of initiatives that they had designed with their integration's bespoke challenges in mind, they would have had to scramble under even more immense time pressures and even fight to counteract what had already gone live.

This process of cultural baselining—what I like to call a cultural diagnostic—emerged as an indispensable throughline across dozens of deals, each of which varied considerably in the business sense but proved revealingly similar in the cultural. The diagnostic has taken many different forms, from a mix of surveys and focus groups to a less formalized series of conversations with folks in pivotal roles, though all are best done well ahead of close. The ideal method varies by context, but whatever the form, the central questions you'll want answers to will remain the same:

- **What is the "real" structure of the organization?** (Not the organizational chart, but how power and influence actually flow within the company)

- **What key processes drive the company?** (The various ways of working, which could vary by level of seniority, as well as by division)
- **How are decisions made?** (Centralized vs. decentralized, command and control vs. consensus-driven)
- **Which people/talent are actually making things happen, and why?** (The "staff sergeants" and influencers in the company)
- **What means are used to motivate people?** (Financial or social incentives, benefits, etc.)
- **What does accountability look like, and how are people held accountable?** (Whether on a team or individual basis, whether people are held accountable evenly across levels of authority, etc.)

This fits well within the category of baselining work for a few reasons. Firstly, and fundamentally speaking, it's critical to get down to a granular level for both your target/partner and your own organization. This level of detail can help dispel harmful misperceptions one side may have of the other, which, if not addressed early on, can entrench feelings of difference.[24] Moreover, it shines a light on any blind spots leaders from either side may have about the cultural reality of their companies. Secondly, as a matter of practice, this work fits naturally within the purview of the IMO and the Integration Teams, who will be working very closely with the people who can best attest to the cultural nuances of their respective areas. And overall, as with more traditional baselines, the cultural diagnostic is meant to provide a clear starting point that will inform the hard work that is to come.

Phase 2: Develop a Clear(er) Vision

"What is possible today that was not possible yesterday?"[25] This provocative question from John Kotter gets right to the heart of the next phase. As the findings from your cultural diagnostic come in, you'll end up with a list of strengths that each company brings to the table (not "good" points and "bad" points, as my McKinsey colleagues point out).[26] The exciting work then becomes figuring out which of the strengths best fit Steerco's vision for the combined company, before devising a way to put those strengths together.

This phase is more involved for some deals than others. In a true merger of equals, for example, an evenly blended Steerco will need to make judicious choices about what elements to (de)prioritize to fulfill their vision for the combined organization. But in the pharma example above, Pharma A's interests lay primarily in its acquisition's R&D. Its cultural diagnostic thus accomplished two ends: first, it allowed Steerco to define clearer targets for the cultural integration between the two companies' respective R&D infrastructures; and second, it validated Steerco's conviction in maintaining Pharma A's existing sales culture as the standard to which all relevant staff who wanted to stay would be expected to adhere.

Effective cultural integration demands specificity, starting from the top. As my experience has corroborated, "culture change is not a goal in itself, but rather a means to achieving a specific business outcome,"[27] which means it's up to Steerco to make the connection between their desired outcomes and the cultural changes needed to realize them. Whether a merger or explicit acquisition, treating culture as ways of doing and investigating those ways through a cultural diagnostic allows a Steerco to more easily identify the specific cultural assets that it wants to "acquire" through a deal in service of its motivating rationale. And with that level of specificity, it can offer concrete grounding to its leaders when it comes time to align them around its vision.

Phase 3: Align Leadership

Here's where things really become more of an art form than an exact science. For all the exceptional planning you and your team have done, the thorough diagnostics you've performed, and even the specific cultural goals you've set, success will depend no less on how well the leaders throughout your organization can serve as stewards of change. While much of the responsibility does lie with the anointed CEO, they alone cannot drive this process "by decree," but they instead must help guide others as contributors and standard bearers.[28] How to secure the alignment that's required, however, varies considerably from leader to leader.

Rather than any strict prescriptions, in this phase, I want to offer a few simple suggestions, each of which targets a different group of leaders. Think of these as corollaries to other integration activities covered in this book, meant to lay the foundation for cultural alignment early in the planning process.

Align Senior Leaders—To Ready the Cultural Cascade

In Chapter Six, I introduced a process of sequential leadership selection called the Personnel Cascade. Starting with senior leadership, this selection process flows downward through the levels of the organization, such that there are enough key leaders in place to lead the merged company from (and to be announced on) Day One. In addition to having numbers at the ready, a second aim is to ensure that those tapped to lead are aligned with the vision for the merged organization. In this way, it's a cascade not only of leadership selection, but also of (preliminary) top-down cultural alignment.

My low-lift suggestion: employ the cultural statement honed over the last few phases as a grounded point of reference, one which your senior leaders can align around, and which they can use to align subsequent layers of leaders. Doug Parker ensured that all of his senior leaders—especially the few he kept on from legacy American Airlines—were bought into the airline as an organization that prioritized operational excellence, a decision that helped set the tone for the entire integration. Following the cascade, those top leaders should emphasize the same cultural reference point to the leaders they decide on. Overall, this means that high-level functional leaders are asked to accept two things in advance as conditions of their appointment: the integration plan they'll be given to implement and the cultural statement they'll be charged with supporting from Day One.

This is, of course, just one small part of a much more complex set of initiatives, but its potential value is multidimensional. First, it sets a clear tone and direction very early in integration planning, which positively reinforces the other streams of integration decision-making going on simultaneously. Second, it helps cement your top layers of culture champions ahead of Day One. And third, it's easily incorporated into existing integration activities. While there's plenty of work still to do, including soliciting input from top management to shape how to communicate and exemplify the new culture, incorporating this cultural element into the Personnel Cascade represents a simple yet efficacious way to build alignment early in integration.

Align the Integration Infrastructure—By Reframing Culture

There's another way to build cultural alignment through existing integration efforts, this time among the Integration Team Leaders, and it starts by simply reframing the work they're preparing to do. If culture lies in how the organization operates, then it's fair to say that their work informs much of how the merged culture will take shape. In defining key processes, protocols, team structures, and more, they're creating more than a pathway to synergy capture—they're establishing much of the substance that will hold up management's cultural messaging. As a result, as part of the IMO's existing efforts to align the Integration Teams around the deal rationale, they should tie the teams' work to the cultural statement and the future of the organization.

In addition to positive encouragement, this can be an effective way to kickstart middle-out cultural change. The most effective efforts I've seen have relied on a multitude of culture champions throughout the organization. Rather than a designation, these champions are respected individuals who fully buy into and exemplify the new culture, such that their peers also come to buy in, too. The Integration Team Leaders are the perfect candidates for this. By reframing their work as shaping the culture under the umbrella of Steerco's specified cultural direction, they can start to serve as both the agents and models of change from within the ranks of the organization.

Align Action—By Tailoring Compensation and Incentives

People will only change if they're provided with the incentives to do so. Leaders of effective change efforts ensure that they pay employees for what they want them to deliver operationally and culturally—and, importantly, that they do away with any rewards tied to actions they want to deprioritize. The cultural statement provides a good starting point in determining the appropriate things to incentivize, while the broader integration plan will inform the specific metrics and rollout of the new compensation system.

Phase 4: Communicate Through Implementation

You also need ways to communicate the new culture to all the people throughout the organization outside the integration planning. Chapter Five's lessons apply here as well: since people will try to make sense of the ongoing change as an unfolding story, integration planners should ask: "What narrative do we want to convey about the culture we're building?" Depending on how you approach the phases above, the cultural statement could effectively frame where that story (the organization) is headed. Since this statement served as the alignment point for senior management and integration leadership, the cultural communications effort should hopefully resonate with the implementation efforts that employees are seeing all around them.

But communicating culture goes beyond words and narratives. In her work on managing cultural change, the late Wharton Professor Sigal Barsade argued that it's not enough to repeatedly (repeatedly, repeatedly, repeatedly…) verbalize the change you want to see—you must role model it for others, as well.[29] Kotter made a similar observation: in a successful cultural change effort, "the leaders did not tell people what culture they wanted. Instead, they were able to demonstrate the behaviors and actions that would result from this culture."[30]

Flipping these observations around reveals another side of the story: people will be watching constantly to see what it is that leaders are role modeling. While you will need a well-conceived formal communications effort, employees will be paying close attention to the informal modes of communication—how you and your culture champions are acting, leading, and living the new culture, and to what degree the conduct that they're witnessing aligns with what they're being told.

Role modeling assumes various forms. Take Parker's decision to adopt American Airlines' headquarters: more than a token gesture, he secured the buy-in to move his senior leaders with him to Dallas, going so far as to announce the church he and his family would be joining to demonstrate they were there to stay. Jim Kilts, meanwhile, conspicuously never bought a home in the Boston area once he became Gilette's CEO. When he announced the deal with P&G, some employees took this as a sign—correctly, as it turned out—that things would soon be shifting towards P&G's center in Cincinnati.

It's impossible to always "be on," but it's much easier to role model the culture you're advocating for when it's authentic and consistent. As you plan your cultural integration and work to get specific about the culture you want, it may help to think in reverse: how will the new leadership operate, and what are the tenets and principles that best encapsulate how they'll be leading?

Phase 5: Watch for Indicators

My experience has taught me that challenges arise much earlier and more often than successes, and frequently in unexpected ways. Is there anything you can do when things deviate from the plan? While determining how to "fix" cultural integration is a uniquely bespoke challenge, you can take steps to prepare yourself for when hurdles arise. Since this effort comes down to your organization's people, create ways to check in with and listen to employees that balance their willingness to speak candidly with management's ability to identify the trends that need addressing. Your customers can also serve as an effective litmus test, even if just by keeping a close eye on satisfaction and referral rates.

At the end of the day, these aren't measurements so much as they are indicators, but by implementing regular means of checking the pulse of the cultural integration effort, you increase your ability to react and respond in the most appropriate way. As Elise Eberwein revealed at the outset of Chapter Four, it took years for legacy American Airlines and US Airways to finally feel like one single entity. In addition to patience, management had to remain vigilant to ensure the entire organization was driving toward a unified culture through the long tail of integration.

KEEPING CULTURE CLOSE TO THE DEAL RATIONALE: TWO CROSS-BORDER CASES

In summary, there isn't one "correct" way to run cultural integration in the same way that there isn't only one "correct" culture for companies to try to cultivate. But in deciding on the kind of culture to strive for and the means to achieve it in the M&A context, leaders can use the rationale guiding their deal as a north star. Starting from that vantage point, built around a business case, integration planners can begin to identify the areas within the soon-to-be combined business most sensitive to the deal's goals (i.e., where to focus cultural integration efforts), as well as the practices and processes most critical to those goals (i.e., what will define the workings of the combined organization). This way of thinking about culture as a necessary companion to the deal rationale can help unlock avenues that may be obscured when culture remains at the abstract level of values, as well as help realign efforts if cultural integration begins to stray.

To close, let's consider two cross-border cases that speak to the importance of the deal rationale to cultural integration. These deals faced significant hurdles and indeed needed to refocus at times, yet they succeeded in creating culturally cohesive organizations by maintaining their deal rationales as the north star.

Integrating IBM PC and Lenovo[31]

When Lenovo announced its purchase of IBM's PC business in December 2004, few industry observers were optimistic. After decades of global dominance, IBM had decided to focus its efforts on IT consulting and sold its PC division, which had been steadily losing market share in the face of fierce competition. This provided Lenovo, then a relative unknown outside of Asia, with a chance to break out on the world stage. But the two cultures seemed virtually opposite: IBM PC was far less formal and rigid—in other words, traditionally American—while Lenovo, largely owned by the Chinese government prior to its emergence as a global superpower, touted a hierarchical ethos evocative of Chairman and cofounder Liu Chuanzi's military background. To complicate matters further, despite Lenovo's goal to "build a Chinese-led international company" through the deal,[32] the negotiated terms stipulated that an IBM leader, Stephen Ward, would serve as CEO, in part because just over half of the combined employees would be coming from IBM.

Initial integration efforts produced mixed results. In retrospect, Chinese leaders' largely "hands-off approach to the US-run PC company" and decision to trust American leaders with base business growth during this period contributed positively to performance.[33] But cultural efforts focused simply on finding ways to communicate and understand each other's perspectives: beyond the significant differences in time zones (well before the normalization of virtual work), few Lenovo employees spoke English and even fewer from IBM spoke Mandarin. Meetings between senior leaders were rare, fraught with misunderstandings, and lacked meaningful connection. Efforts were made to investigate employees' opinions, though questionnaires and interviews focused predominantly on which management styles they thought were better and the problems they expected people from each side to experience. After a year of essentially continued separation, new CEO William Amelio (another former IBMer) increased the frequency of senior meetings and asked that all senior managers use English as the official work language, policies which pushed some Chinese leaders to leave.

Beginning in 2006, Lenovo initiated a new cultural effort that brought leaders together in person on a more regular basis. As a result, Chinese and American leaders began to understand not just *that* they were different, but how the ways in which they communicated, led, and made decisions (and followed them) differed with more nuance. By 2008, the company had achieved significant gains, leading some insiders to hail the cultural integration as a success. But in the wake of the financial crisis that unfolded the following year, much of that strong performance evaporated, and long-time Chinese leaders were left questioning the state of the company.

It took renewed attempts in 2009 and 2010, this time returning to Liu's initial vision for the deal, to create a more cohesive cultural identity. While acknowledging the value his American counterparts had brought, he argued that Lenovo had gradually shifted away from its prior focus on formal planning and execution to a culture that valorized talk but didn't do enough to secure follow through. In pushing Lenovo to bounce back from the financial crisis and emerge as a distinctly Chinese multinational, he inspired an effort that created a new objectives-based evaluation system and incentive structure, as well as laid off roughly 10% of its employees (which included parting ways with a number of American senior leaders like Amelio). Though not an easy process, this campaign focused on incentivizing behavioral change, rather than just seeking mutual understanding, and galvanized the company en route to becoming the leader in global PC sales for the first time in 2013.[34]

Integrating Beam Suntory[35]

In January 2014, the Japanese beverages group Suntory acquired Beam Inc. for a handsome $16 billion. Suntory's whiskeys had dominated the Japanese market, but with little global presence and fears around Japan's aging (and shrinking) population, the company's leaders thought that acquisition offered the best way to expand. Beam, who already had a distribution agreement with Suntory and was in the midst of a resurgence in the United States, emerged as the prime candidate. Cognizant of the failures of past transnational transactions and pressed to pay down the hefty debt it had incurred to make the purchase, Suntory started with a hands-off, "watch and learn" approach that vested a significant amount of control in Beam's existing management: CEO Matthew Shattock and his team would run the new Beam Suntory from its existing headquarters in suburban Deerfield, Illinois, and would even gain managerial oversight over Suntory's Japanese spirits business. For the first few months of integration, Suntory's aim was not just to maintain Beam's strengths and cultural identity, but to import some of the cultural elements that had made Beam a global brand back to Japan.

Following Takeshi Niinami's appointment as President and CEO in October, however, Suntory began to shift its approach. Months of careful observation and patience had made clear the strengths each side brought to the table—now, it was time to capitalize on them. After restructuring the corporate governance such that Shattock now reported to Niinami, Suntory began implementing changes, including adopting Beam's risk management practices, implementing a more rigid financial reporting structure within the American operation, moving Beam's headquarters from the suburbs to Chicago, and applying Japanese process optimization (*kaizen*) to Beam's production. Despite Beam's anxiety and even the loss of some legacy employees with the headquarters' relocation, Suntory navigated the cultural integration by focusing on their shared identity as craftsmen: under the aegis of *monozukuri* (craftsmanship), Beam came to embrace Suntory's attention to detail and quality control. And at the same time, the Beam side felt like a valued partner in leading Suntory into the global market and teaching its distillers about the nuances of bourbon.

Though the initial slow pace contributed to Suntory's success, the real key was in how they built around the deal rationale and focused on behaviors. Delegating authority to Beam allowed Suntory to build its global capacity, while also allowing it to identify the collective, aligned strengths that could take their combined endeavors to the next level. Suntory leaders then role-modeled the behaviors and practices that they wanted the entire organization to embody, importantly through the lens of quality craftsmanship that both sides could buy into.

ACTION ITEMS IN REVIEW

- **Get specific about the ways of working that define each side.** While espoused values are important, it's how those values are espoused—in leadership styles, approaches to decision-making, key processes—that really defines how similar two groups of people are. From expanded diligence to cultural diagnostic work, the earlier you can develop a detailed cultural baseline, the better your integration planning can target the areas that matter most for your combined organization.

- **Develop a concrete cultural vision that stems from your deal rationale.** Cultural integration doesn't exist in a vacuum—the changes you implement to realize the deal's rationale necessarily shape the culture of the new organization. If the cultural diligence and baselining work provides the detailed topographical map, the deal rationale represents the compass that guides integration planning in the cultural direction best suited for the deal.

- **Make it an organization-wide effort.** The CEO and senior management must lead by example, but without support from throughout the organization, culture is unlikely to change. It's critical to activate and lean on culture champions as part of this effort: by tying their work to culture creation and aligning them around Steerco's cultural vision, the IMO can help turn Integration Team Leaders into advocates for the new culture among their colleagues.

- **Regularly look for indicators.** Look for signs from within and outside the company that speak to employee morale and engagement with the proposed cultural direction. Since happiness and satisfaction can be hard to measure, consider developing cultural benchmarks based on the working styles or outputs you want to foster and tracking how your people are doing in relation to them.

CHAPTER NINE

WHEN ONE JOURNEY ENDS... COMPLETING THE INTEGRATION— AND PREPARING FOR THE NEXT

W hen do you stop integrating? Compared to integration planning and the first 100 days of execution—their sheer intensity and the vast amount of attention they receive—it's easy to think of the end of the effort more as a whimper than a bang. Unlike announcing the deal, there's no big celebration or clear milestone. If anything, the end may feel like an anticlimactic transition back to business as usual after months of exertion, rather than a culminating moment of catharsis. But despite this impression, how you wind down the integration effort can affect the present deal as well as influence how your organization handles future integrations.

In order to plan for the end, you need to know what "finished" looks like—the problem being that integration contains multiple transitions that we can consider end points (some of which are more final than others). Dismissing the IMO, for example, only means that business units are well enough along the way to execute the plans they've accepted and no longer need additional tracking. So, while it does signify the end of integration hallmarks like the Parallel Process and the start of a new normal, past that point, it could still take months for systems to integrate, and even years past that for a unified culture to emerge, as is the case for countless mergers. By then, you might not even realize the end point has been reached.

The first goal of this chapter is to make it easier for you to determine when the integration effort is complete, as well as to understand what that really means. Rather than asking when integration *should* end, let's instead get specific about what the final stages of the IMO's tracking cadence often entail and encounter, including some subtle(r) signs to look out for that qualitatively signal that the effort is reaching its natural conclusion.

The end of one effort is also a great opportunity to prepare for the next one. These preparations begin by conducting an impartial review that memorializes your integration work, debriefs key decisions, and distills valuable lessons for future use, including takeaways on the techniques, technologies, and even advisors that took part in the effort. But your options for future readiness extend beyond memorialization and review: as we get into the tradeoffs of investing in internal capabilities versus bringing in outside help, I'll also introduce a broad array of other materials and processes that an effort can leave behind to build an institutional knowledge base in service of future deals to come.

A SIGN OF THE TIMES: INDICATIONS OF AN EFFORT NEARING COMPLETION

The IMO was always meant to be temporary. By now, maybe between three and six months into the implementation, their work has both changed and wound down considerably from the time of their launch. As we saw in Chapter Seven, once the organization transitioned into integration implementation from Day One, the major portion of their work shifted from synergy planning to monitoring progress and coordinating activities (and a few more discussed later in this chapter), as in Figure 9.1, on the next page. At the same time, most (if not all) of its members likely moved from working full-time on the integration to part-time as they assumed new leadership roles in the combined organization. With the weight of their added responsibilities and the growing sentiment within the company to get back to business as usual, the question has become: when is the right time to bring their work to a formal end?

First, a word of caution: dissolving the IMO too early in the implementation can risk unraveling the effort. Particularly when IMO members are assuming senior roles within the combined company, the new CEO may worry about their ability to juggle both sets of responsibilities effectively, especially given their likelihood for exhaustion following the intense planning effort. Under these conditions, CEOs might be tempted to release the IMO members within the first several weeks of the implementation, before integration targets have been fully "baked into" business units' formal operational plans. But no matter how strong this concern may be, the early stages of implementation are when clear direction, structured tracking, and discipline are needed most. In other words, discontinuing the IMO "too soon" can take the pressure off proper synergy alignment, acceptance, and tracking before it's truly clear whether teams are firmly off in the right direction.[1]

Figure 9.1   A simplified timeline of major IMO milestones.

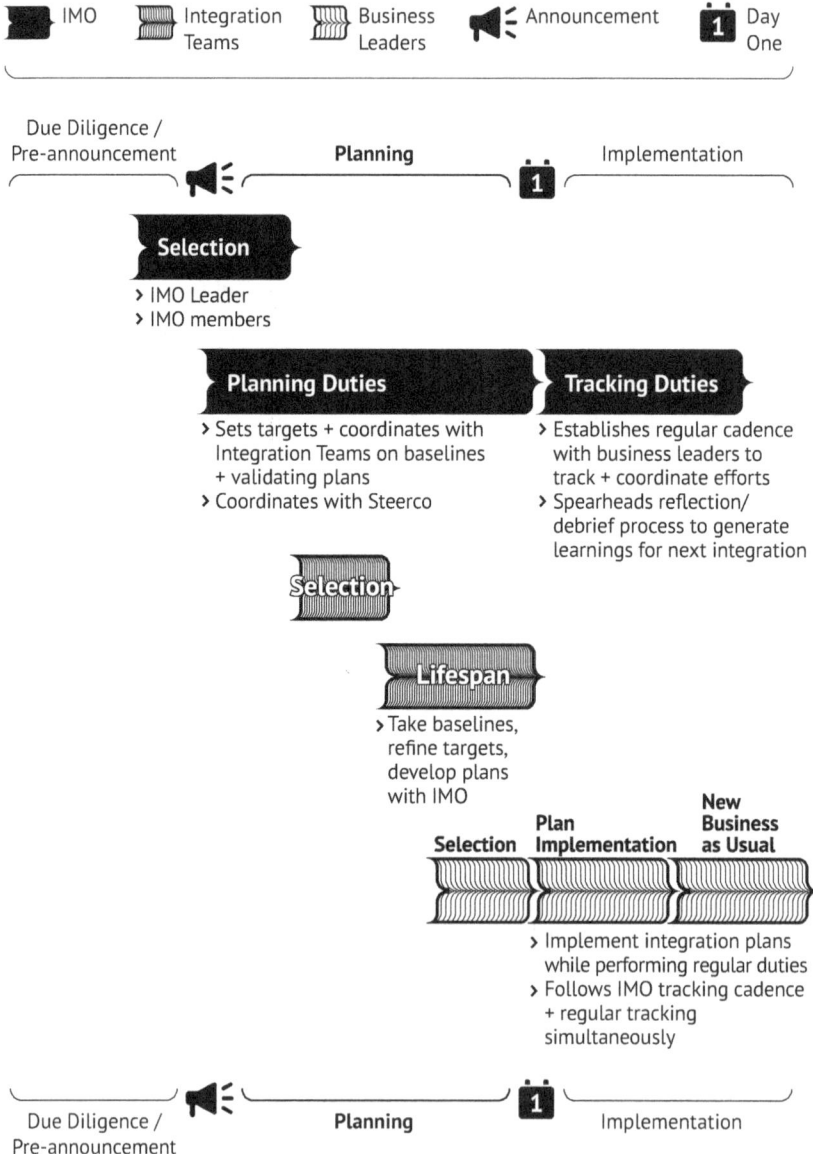

Determining the appropriate moment to discontinue the IMO first depends on the progress that business/functional units make toward the goals developed by the Integration Teams. Ideally, during their planning work with the IMO, each team will have identified the target end state for their unit, but rarely will they need the IMO's continued oversight all the way until they reach that end state. Instead, teams should be allowed to "graduate" from IMO reporting once they demonstrate a clear path to meet their integration objectives *and* no other interdependent workstream needs to actively coordinate with them,[2] after which point the responsibility for achieving the remaining integration-related goals shifts to line operations and/or key functional leaders.

Naturally, some units will accomplish this sooner than others. During the American Airlines merger, for example, it took longer to figure out how to combine each airline's loyalty points than it did to streamline cargo. Rather than force them to continue attending the regular integration meetings, they were allowed to exit the IMO reporting cadence. This makes shutting down the IMO much more a selective process than a single culminating moment.

Business leaders will often make it known once the IMO cadence has diminished past a point of value. In short, they'll get frustrated with the IMO and the need to continually report progress both to them and to their operational bosses. Indeed, this antagonism results naturally from the Parallel Process: past a certain point, many leaders perceive integration tracking as a burden that eats into their ability to lead their part of the base business. The IMO need not acquiesce at the first signs of tension, but the interpersonal dynamic can act as a helpful litmus test in further gauging a unit's progress and the need for continued additional tracking (particularly useful for CEOs who feel tempted to keep the IMO on for up to a year or more).

MEMORIALIZATION AND REFLECTION: DEBRIEFING AS PREPARATION

As the tracking cadence winds down to a close, the IMO can turn to its final set of responsibilities: priming for the company's next integration. Having just led a massive transformation effort, the members of this team have gained a tremendous amount of experiential learning that will prove valuable not only to them personally, but also more importantly to the organization going forward. How, and to what extent, it can utilize this learning, however, depends on the ways in which the IMO frames its key learnings.

Just as the bespoke nature of integration influences how to plan for it, so too does it shape the kinds of takeaways it produces. Contrary to expectation, integration experience doesn't necessarily translate to integration success: in what Timothy Galpin and Mark Herndon call the "deal-count paradox," there's a surprising number of frequent acquirers (in the range of even 100+ deals) who fail to realize expected value time and again, seemingly counter to the experience they've acquired.[3] Acquirers who think primarily in terms of first-order takeaways—"It worked great to staff the IMO this way"; "It wasn't helpful to hold an offsite launch for the Integration Teams"; and so on—are particularly susceptible to this paradox, because first-order lessons aren't always applicable across deal contexts. Rather, by additionally distilling second-order learnings from their experience, leaders can help future IMO members better anticipate and address the issues they may run into.

One way to structure the reflection process is through a document that does the following:

- **Memorializes** all decisions and outcomes while memories are fresh (descriptive timeline)
- **Reviews** comprehensively and objectively all achievements and mistakes in a non-evaluative way (first-order takeaways)

174

- **Distills** high-level learnings from the achievements and mistakes (second-order takeaways)
- **Recommends** changes to the IMO/integration process based on overall lessons learned (applied learning)

This isn't a "playbook" because it's not meant to chart a set course for your next IMO to run. In fact, the ambiguity that defines today's landscape has made relying on playbooks much more prone to missteps than seeking out insights to cultivate a more adaptive and agile mindset.[4] Instead, think of this document as a primer to inform the future IMO of past trouble spots, tip them off to potential patterns, and recommend potential improvements as they plan for the next integration. The goal for this document, as a compilation of all the "aha"s from the current integration, is to become one of the first resources your next IMO turns to.

Empowered Insight Gathering

This memorialization and review process works best when it involves people at different levels. Since the strength of this document depends on the quality of the insights generated, it's key to rely on interviews and surveys to collect as many perspectives as possible. More than just the experiences of the IMO and Steerco, this document can capture thoughts from senior management, business leaders, members of the Integration Teams, employees in areas particularly affected by the integration, and even the consultants who supported the engagement. A helpful goal is to collect a variety of viewpoints that reflect the nuances of the integration effort, as well as perspectives that are easier to overlook from the vantage of the IMO (who may miss the forest for the trees).

Who handles this work can vary by institution. In many cases, especially for companies with limited internal integration capabilities, it falls to the IMO, though increasingly it may become an added responsibility for corporate development, strategy, or even a standing Project Management

Office. Which of these is the most appropriate could depend on the size and strategic complexity of the deal, whether it was more process-oriented, or simply how a company allocates resources among these functions. Regardless, it should be a dedicated and prioritized effort carried out by a team that is familiar with the deal rationale and empowered to speak with key leaders from the integration throughout the organization.

This combination of traits raises another option: consultants. The work that the consulting team was brought on to support will have already connected them with the very people throughout the organization needed for such a review, and their third-party perspective will lend a level of objectivity that can be hard to achieve from internal teams. In fact, this kind of after-action review, complete with recommendations, is just the kind of work that consultants are excited to do—and often precisely what the IMO members want to put off as they transition fully into their role in the newly combined organization.

In his *Mergers & Acquisitions Integration Handbook*, Scott Whitaker dedicates two chapters to the integration feedback process and the creation of a document like this.[5] Though he adopts the "playbook" approach, he nevertheless offers a helpful range of elements the IMO (or other governing body) might consider, including in its memorialization and debrief effort.

DEVELOPING CAPABILITIES: BUILD INTERNALLY OR BRING IN OUTSIDE HELP?

The closing stages of integration offer a decision point and opportunity for later endeavors: how much should your organization develop and maintain internal capabilities for future integrations? This debate has evolved considerably since the start of my career, back when just forming a dedicated

IMO was an innovation. Apart from General Electric, which was then the rare exception to staff its high-potentials on the integration effort,[6] the dominant position was to rely largely on outside help. Since M&A transactions were such specialized endeavors, CEOs felt reluctant to dedicate too many resources to what they would eventually hire consultants for anyway.

But that trend has changed alongside M&A's increasingly prominent role in corporate strategy. As companies become hungrier for disruption opportunities, they're dedicating an increasing amount of financial and human capital to transformation programs and increasingly staffing them with highly experienced, full-time leadership over third-party help, as a 2025 Deloitte study has shown.[7] At the same time, there's been a gradual shift in perception around integration as more people come to see supporting the integration effort as an opportunity for career advancement, rather than a time to apply elsewhere.[8] Now, the paradigm leans much more toward investing in internal capabilities like a Transformation Office to handle M&A and integration rather than perpetually hiring outsiders who won't know the ins and outs of the company.

Taking up the mantle of the Project Management Offices of the last several decades, the Transformation Office is a team responsible for driving internal transformation efforts. Often headed by a Chief Transformation Officer, it's aligned according to the mandate of the CEO and is supposed to act as a "single source of truth" for all efforts through rigorous planning, tracking, and, if necessary, intervention.[9] Its oversight across a wide range of transformation efforts gives it a broad field of vision that can help it to weave complex initiatives like cultural integration more seamlessly into the bigger picture. All the same, depending on the scale of existing efforts, its extensive purview can also act as a limitation to diving deep into the weeds like a dedicated team can.

That's why, even amid this shift, outside help can still play a vital role. Beyond the lawyers and bankers you need to arrange a deal, it likely still makes sense to rely on the specialized expertise of consultants to determine things like accurate baselines. And since it takes time not just to establish, for example, a Transformation Office, but to develop in its members the know-how and experience to be effective, you might consider bringing in strategic advisors to work alongside them on their first integrations. That way, you provide a practical pathway for those who are intimately familiar with your organization's ways to gain invaluable experience while minimizing the risk of throwing them in too quickly.

Small Steps Toward Readiness

For organizations looking to make the first steps toward integration readiness (or just selectively build on existing resources), there are a few time-tested approaches. Each of these focuses on the capabilities that most influence the creation and preservation of value in integration. And simplest of all, any of these can be developed by the consultants your organization has brought on in support of the integration—though it takes the dedication and effort of leadership to ensure their independent continuation once the consultants' efforts have concluded. While the appropriate level of investment is for your organization to determine, any one of these can be feasibly included in your consultants' existing engagement:

- **Integration Team Playbooks.** The "playbook" language feels appropriate here because these documents have a particularly granular function. Rather than sketch takeaways for a future IMO, these playbooks catalogue the processes and tools for future Integration Teams to develop their integration plans.
- **Processes to Capture Learnings.** If your organization needs help undertaking the reflection and memorialization process, consultants are well prepared to support in the present, as well as to help create structures to build on and maintain institutional memory in the future.

- **Deal Synergy/Financial Management Systems.** These are streamlined financial systems for the development of baselines, as well as the tracking of synergy obtainment and their costs.
- **Functional Readiness Materials.** Essentially primers and reference guides to get people up to speed, these materials describe the typical functional activities required for integration, and the resources dedicated to them.
- **Integration "Boot Camps."** These can range from workshops targeting foundational skills (e.g., pattern recognition, interdependency management), which can be run in between integrations, to intensive programs designed to launch Integration Teams and acquaint them with each other, the integration approach, their responsibilities, work plans, and the relevant lexicon.
- **Integration Mentors/Guides.** Institutional memory isn't limited to reference guides and materials. One of the most effective (and simple) support systems is to ask individuals to serve as resources for IMO and Integration Team members according to their prior integration expertise, whether that's according to function, geography, business content, or otherwise.

THE LONG TAIL OF POST-IMO INTEGRATION

Once all business units have exited the integration cadence, the postmortem review is complete, the IMO has been dissolved, and its members have either assumed their new roles in or left the organization, is integration finally over? In a very formal sense, yes: with the scaffolds of the integration apparatus removed, the company can finally focus its full attention on "business as usual." But reality is rarely so straightforward. For many deals, especially large and more complex ones, it can take far longer for the components of the formerly independent companies to become fully integrated. Elise Eberwein told us as much in Chapter Four: for years, the "new" American Airlines had to run legacy systems in parallel while teams in IT, HR, and elsewhere worked to create new integrated solutions, not to mention the time it took for legacy identities to gel into a culturally unified whole. In this sense, post-integration "business as usual" really constitutes a "new normal," rather than a return to affairs pre-integration.

The road to complete integration is long and can extend until after the integration effort itself has disappeared in the rearview mirror. Taking up the mantle left by the IMO, it's now up to the combined organization's leadership to ensure its cohesion and to remain focused on realizing the aspirations behind the preceding months of intensive effort. It will take continued effort to ensure things come together and work as one—until it's time for the next deal to start the process over again.

ACTION ITEMS IN REVIEW

- **Look for the subtle indications of an integration effort nearing completion.** Functional leaders, shouldering the weight of added reporting from the Parallel Process, often signal (though not always verbally) when their unit is ready to exit the IMO's cadence.
- **Conduct a thorough postmortem review of the integration effort.** Employing interviews and surveys, create a document that memorializes key decisions, distills essential learnings, and offers recommendations based on the effort that future IMOs can use as a primer for their subsequent integration.
- **Consider developing internal capabilities for future integrations.** Taking into account factors like existing capabilities, the experience from this integration effort, the role M&A plays in

your organization's growth strategy, and other ongoing/intended change efforts, determine whether it's appropriate to invest in targeted skill-building efforts or more substantial initiatives like a Transformation Office—and whether you can include them in your ongoing integration.

EPILOGUE

REFLECTING ON A CAREER AS AN INTEGRATION ADVISOR

T he arc of this book has traced the work of numerous operators: whether the CEO, the members of the IMO, Integration Team leaders, business unit heads, or otherwise, decision-makers have taken center stage. But there's been another side to the story running along in the background. The lessons I've learned around post-merger integration have materialized through my work as an advisor, ranging from my formative days as a junior consultant to my most high-stakes engagements as a senior partner and my learning gained as a professor. In developing this book, I had the opportunity to reflect not only on the lessons I've learned and the advice I've given, but also on my own position as a contributor to integration. Through this reflection, I came to the realization that there's another set of learnings concealed in the advisor's vantage on integration. This Epilogue emerged as an attempt to distill the core of that learning in a way that supplements the rest of the book's primary focus on the operator perspective.

These closing thoughts center on the nature of advisory work and integration's overlooked relational potential. More so than in the rest of the book, this section speaks directly to the advisor's role and experience, and in that way, it offers perspective for consultants at all levels, whether specializing in integration work or otherwise, on the nature of client service. At the same time, just as an advisor's work can't be separated from the client it's meant to serve, this short chapter also tries to pull back the curtain for the operators to help them make the most of their advisory relationships and even use integration as a proving ground for longer-term advising. Overall, it tries to address two main questions: What makes an advisor versus an operator versus a consultant? And what is it about integration that makes it such a special opportunity to build meaningful client–advisor relationships?

OPERATORS, ADVISORS, AND THE MUTUAL CHALLENGE (AND OPPORTUNITY) IN INTEGRATION

What's the difference between an operator and an advisor? In my time as an educator, I've worked with hundreds of students who've had to wrangle with this question. Harvard's MBA program foregrounds general management and leadership frequently from the perspective of impactful executives, visionaries, founders—operators—as they face down an exceedingly difficult decision. Through the lens of these protagonists, our students develop the convictions that inform how they might one day respond to the challenging decisions they'll have to make. But this kind of conviction doesn't entirely correlate to those whose careers will depend on how well they help others make such decisions. These aspiring advisors need a

184

different kind of perspective, one that centers on enriching the perspective of another and guiding them toward their success.

I first learned about the distinction from my father. After fleeing fascist Italy with his father in 1939, Eugene Fubini built his career in service to the United States, starting as a scientific researcher contributing to the Allied war effort. In 1963, President Kennedy appointed him to the position of Assistant Secretary of Defense following a distinguished stint at the Pentagon. But despite the heights he reached as an operator, it was his role heading the Defense Science Board for over two decades that he considered most valued. He took great pride in his work as a consultant in the purest sense—someone whom many would seek out for counsel—and he felt that he was able to produce far more meaningful impact as an advisor to successive generations of American leadership than he was even as a high-ranking political appointee himself.

In summing up the north star of that work, he frequently recalled an anecdote concerning two men of considerable influence in Kennedy-era Washington. As the story went, Joseph Alsop, the renowned columnist for *The Washington Post*, was speaking with Ted Sorenson, who had served as Kennedy's speechwriter, special counsel, and advisor. The two friends, grief-stricken in the wake of the President's assassination, had seen the very nature of their world change in an instant. It was at this crucial inflection point that Alsop urged Sorensen to stay the course and continue the work that had so greatly contributed to the aims of the administration. For though the President was the one to implement matters of policy, it had been the advisor's counsel that "strengthened his arm and extended his reach" at a crucially dire point in the Cold War.

For management consultants, putting this wisdom into practice means acting as an "alternative idea generator" based on insights generally not seen by senior management. Often the instinct is to impart knowledge, given the breadth of experience and context that consultants from leading firms are expected to have. But the work of an advisor is to take the position and needs of the client into account and, using one's experience and objectivity, to craft a set of feasible options that the client can act upon, based on their priorities and appetite for risk.

Integration advising complicates that picture. Facing extreme time pressures and a highly integrated set of decision points, the job often requires *narrowing* options to keep the client on track and focused. In fact, more so than any other kind of engagement I undertook, supporting integration demands an operator's mindset, one which balances the fundamental tradeoffs of time, talent, and capital, and decides on—or at least strongly recommends—swift action accordingly.

Without question, supporting integration formed me into a better advisor. The operator perspectives required by this kind of work broadened my point of view and allowed me to better appreciate the challenging positions my clients would find themselves in (and meant working extremely closely with management personalities, as well). In this way, it also alerted me to a dual possibility. For consultants, especially in the earlier stages of their career, supporting integration can hone the entirety of their advisory toolkit and expose them to the leaders—or future leaders—who could shape the trajectory of their service to come. By the same token, integration also provides operators the conditions to work with and identify the kind of advisor who might serve them far beyond the current engagement—provided they know what to look for.

AN ADVISOR'S RESPONSIBILITIES

The consulting industry has had its fair share of problems (and challenges of late), but at the heart of the work lies the commitment to professionalism and client service. As such, the fundamental responsibilities of an advisor transcend the specifics of any engagement: in "extending the reach" of a client, an advisor should be prepared to offer support in any way a client may need. That starts by working to understand the client and their needs in their own terms, a premise that takes on heightened significance when advising on integration.

In the mid-1990s, once I had begun to build my reputation as an integration advisor, I was called in to help with the integration between two major partner-based firms. Like so many of the examples in this book, these two firms did a lot of the same work, but their cultures were radically different. So I spearheaded a thorough effort to get to the heart of these differences—how each side understood themselves and each other, how their approach to client work and the kinds of clients they worked with differed, how they defined the quality of their engagements—and used that as the basis for a showcase of how these two firms could come together and produce results. Heading into a meeting with the combined leadership team, I already had visions of the confetti and cheers I'd receive after giving them the good news: the integration could achieve a 20–30% increase in partner gain! (Provided they attended to the litany of things I'd say they could, should, and would need to do.)

I was met with a row of indifferent faces. It was the senior partner tapped to lead the combined firm who broke the silence: "You know, David, I think I speak for everybody here. That sounds like a lot of work—and rather tedious work—and I'm not so sure we really care that much about partner gain. We really like the sort of lifestyle and approach we have, and your plan is asking us to do something we don't really want to do."

An advisor's first responsibility—taking the steps to understand the real reasons and aspirations behind the deal—I had failed to uphold. I certainly had what I thought was a strong intuition: after all, why else would they have gone through with a transaction of that scale if not for the chance at huge partner gain? But I was wrong, and I had let my own vision lead the way. The lesson that emerged here has stuck with me ever since, and it arguably sparked the thinking around which this book is built—around the centrality of the deal rationale not only to the integration effort, but also to the advisor's support of their client.

Once an advisor understands the true reasons for the deal, they must then help the client stay laser-focused on them. No matter how many suggestions and advance warnings this book has given to help prepare you for the gauntlet of extreme prioritization that is integration, filtering out the signal from the noise is exceedingly difficult. CEOs naturally want to make decisions, and integrations abound with decisions. Recognizing this, an advisor's job is to keep the client on the critical path, as well as to help them understand what the critical path is and why it's important. That way, the client is better equipped for their next integration effort—whether they decide to bring the advisor back in an official capacity or not.

Nowhere is this more salient than the difficult decisions around people and culture. It's admittedly hard to grasp the full range of challenges here without firsthand experience: the gap between recognizing *that* there will be overlaps to eliminate in pursuit of synergy capture and the reality of letting people go in a rapid and thoughtful way may as well be a chasm, to say nothing of everything else covered in Chapter Eight (and the many more things that had to be left out). It's part of the advisor's role to get management to face up to all this work at the "right" time and in the "right" way—whatever that might be according to the goals for the deal.

THE START OF SOMETHING MORE

Consultants wanting to specialize in integration must reckon with a handful of tradeoffs. To begin with, these engagements rarely contribute positively to work–life balance: more than just forcing long hours, they demand a considerable level of nonstop intensity and exertion. The stakes are high, the work hard, and the challenges numerous. From the perspective of advancing within the firm, these engagements don't really translate to the usual metrics for evaluation: you're usually not the one responsible for bringing in and developing the client, but instead perceived as a functional specialist looped in for an existing client, a distinction that may cost you when you're considered for advancement. Much like a relief pitcher in baseball, you're brought in under immense pressure to close out what others started, if not like a firefighter called to douse growing flames.

But for all the tradeoffs and challenges of integration, it was the depth of the relationships I was able to build that kept me coming back. To an extent unlike any other kind of engagement, supporting integration allowed me to spend substantive, meaningful time with CEOs and their senior team in a way that felt like a true partnership. In some cases, these bonds of partnership developed into deep advisory relationships that lasted far beyond the engagement through the twists and turns of our careers. This wasn't the case every time, of course, but a trend nevertheless emerged that demonstrated the extent to which integration could serve as a proving ground for long-term relationships of trust.

That trust first stems from the degree of shared exertion toward a shared objective. The same pressures that pushed me to think like an operator also brought me closer together with my clients: with extremely tight timeframes and countless competing demands, the difference between success and failure hinged much more closely on the efficacy of our partnership. The team may have put themselves in a winning position, but victory was not guaranteed—as the reliever, I still had to do my part to help the team close out. And while the dynamics varied from engagement to engagement, and some styles gelled better than others, the most impactful proved to be when the sense of partnership emerged strongest.

At the same time, the extreme conditions of integration also facilitate another central aspect of advising: pushing when the moment calls for it, even if it's uncomfortable. Feeling the pressures from their firms' up-or-out culture and their clients' expectations for return on their (often considerable) investment, many of my students harbor uncertainties around how to navigate this part of their advisory role. But with tact, thoughtful framing, and an understanding of the client's aspirations and circumstances, an advisor serves to add the most value when they speak truth to power.

Still, even late in your career, this can be very hard to do—and sometimes not without consequence. Some years ago, I was asked to help a senior team as they planned for their upcoming integration, one they expected to be quite logistically complex. Though the deal had considerable cross-border implications, the conversation focused almost entirely on addressing potential issues in the United States. As the meeting neared what felt like its end point, I decided to ask the question, and the team indicated they expected the remaining pieces to fall into place once they got things settled in the heartland. But I had seen this scenario play out before (and not in the deal's favor), so I decided to push one step further for a more specific plan and, having clearly spoiled the mood, expected not to be invited back.

After some weeks of radio silence, I received a call from the CEO. It's true that my pushing had dampened the mood and even caused some ire. At the same time, it helped encourage the senior leaders to investigate the situation in more detail—and there was some surprise at what they found. The team would have found out eventually, but the time-sensitive, sequential demands of integration exacerbate the penalties of oversight and missed opportunities. Serving as an advisor meant raising the issue in the hope of best serving the client's aspirations, even if that meant parting ways over a disconnect in perspective.

NOTES

INTRODUCTION

1. Clayton M. Christensen, Richard Alton, Curtis Rising, and Andrew Waldeck, "The Big Idea: The New M&A Playbook," *Harvard Business Review*, March 2011, https://hbr.org/2011/03/the-big-idea-the-new-ma-playbook (accessed March 16, 2025).
2. David Harding, Dale Stafford, and Suzanne Kumar, "How Companies Got So Good at M&A," Bain & Company, April 2024, https://www.bain.com/insights/how-companies-got-so-good-at-m-and-a (accessed March 17, 2025); Harvard Business Review, "A Better Approach to Mergers and Acquisitions," *Harvard Business Review*, May 1, 2024, https://hbr.org/2024/05/a-better-approach-to-mergers-and-acquisitions (accessed March 17, 2025).
3. Robert Eccles, Kersten Lanes, and Thomas Wilson, "Are You Paying Too Much for That Acquisition?" *Harvard Business Review*, July 1, 1999, https://hbr.org/1999/07/are-you-paying-too-much-for-that-acquisition (accessed March 18, 2025); Mark Sirower and Jeffery Weirens, *The Synergy Solution: How Companies Win the Mergers and Acquisitions Game* (Boston, MA: Harvard Business Review Press, 2022); Ayse Karaevli and Serden Özcan, "Why Some CFOs Make Better M&A Deals," *MIT Sloan Management Review*, May 26, 2022, https://sloanreview.mit.edu/article/why-some-cfos-make-better-ma-deals (accessed March 18, 2025).
4. Christensen et al. (2011). A major tenet of McKinsey's M&A advisory practice is convincing clients that these transactions are enablers of strategy, not strategy themselves: "M&A Strategy & Due Diligence," McKinsey & Company, 2025, https://www.mckinsey.com/capabilities/m-and-a/how-we-help-clients/m-and-a-strategy-due-diligence (accessed March 18, 2025).

5. Harding et al. (2024); Harvard Business Review (2024).
6. Alan Lewis and Dan McKone, "So Many M&A Deals Fail Because Companies Overlook This Simple Strategy," *Harvard Business Review*, May 10, 2016, https://hbr.org/2016/05/so-many-ma-deals-fail-because-companies-overlook-this-simple-strategy (accessed January 9, 2025).
7. "Robert A. Iger," *The Economic Club of New York*, October 24, 2019, https://www.econclubny.org/legacyarchive/-/blogs/robert-a-iger (accessed March 16, 2025).
8. Jordan Novet, "Satya Nadella's First Decade as Microsoft CEO was Defined by Cloud. What's Next?" *CNBC* online, February 4, 2024, https://www.cnbc.com/2024/02/04/microsoft-ceo-satya-nadella-hits-10-year-anniversary.html (accessed March 16, 2025).

CHAPTER 1

1. Duncan Angwin, "Merger and Acquisition Typologies: A Review," in *The Handbook of Mergers and Acquisitions*, eds. David Faulkner, Satu Teerikangas, and Richard Joseph (Oxford: Oxford University Press, 2012), 40–70.
2. See also: Robert T. Uhlaner and Andrew S. West, "Running a Winning M&A Shop," McKinsey & Company, March 1, 2008, https://www.mckinsey.com/capabilities/strategy-and-corporate-finance/our-insights/running-a-winning-m-and-a-shop (accessed March 25, 2025); Marc Goedhart, Tim Koller, and David Wessels, "The Six Types of Successful Acquisitions," McKinsey & Company, May 10, 2017, https://www.mckinsey.com/capabilities/strategy-and-corporate-finance/our-insights/the-six-types-of-successful-acquisitions (accessed March 17, 2025).
3. Jared Reiger and Nidhi Meppadan, *Why M&A Transactions Fail and How to Drive Successful Integration in AP* (Boston Consulting Group, September 2024), 6–8, https://web-assets.bcg.com/05/2c/2877048145f6801138d1134d5a3c/why-m-a-transactions-fail-and-how-to-drive-successful-integration-in-ap.pdf (accessed March 25, 2025).
4. James McLetchie and Andy West, "Beyond Risk Avoidance: A McKinsey Perspective on Creating Transformational Value from Mergers," in *Perspectives on Merger Integration* (McKinsey & Company, June 2010), 11, https://www.mckinsey.com/client_service/organization/latest_thinking/~/media/1002A11EEA4045899124B917EAC7404C.ashx.
5. Michael Barbaro, "As a Boss, Carly Fiorina Was a Contradictory Figure at Hewlett-Packard," *The New York Times*, October 26, 2015, https://www.nytimes.com/2015/10/27/us/politics/carly-fiorina-was-contradictory-figure-at-hewlett-packard.html (accessed August 20, 2024).

6. Carol J. Loomis, "Why Carly's Big Bet Is Failing," *Fortune*, February 7, 2005, https://fortune.com/article/why-carlys-big-bet-is-failing-fortune-classics-2005 (accessed August 19, 2024).

7. Dawn Kawamoto, "Judge Dismisses HP Merger Lawsuit," *CNET*, June 1, 2002, https://www.cnet.com/tech/tech-industry/judge-dismisses-hp-merger-lawsuit (accessed August 20, 2024).

8. "Michael Capellas' Next Move," *Forbes*, November 11, 2002 (updated June 6, 2013), https://www.forbes.com/2002/11/11/cx_ld_1111hp.html (accessed August 29, 2024).

9. Rob Wright, "The HP-Compaq Merger: Partners Reflect 10 Years Later," *CRN*, September 8, 2011, https://www.crn.com/news/mobility/231601009/the-hp-compaq-merger-partners-reflect-10-years-later (accessed August 19, 2024).

10. Pui-Wing Tam, "Hewlett-Packard Posts a Loss in First Results After Merger," *The Wall Street Journal*, August 28, 2002, https://www.wsj.com/articles/SB1030461863895147395 (accessed April 2, 2025).

11. Brian Dinneen, Christine Johnson, and Alex Liu, "Post-close Excellence in Large-deal M&A," McKinsey & Company, June 29, 2021, https://www.mckinsey.com/capabilities/m-and-a/our-insights/post-close-excellence-in-large-deal-m-and-a (accessed March 25, 2025); Brian Dinneen, Christine Johnson, Becky Kaetzler, and Alex Liu, "In Conversation: Four Keys to Merger Integration Success," McKinsey & Company, October 12, 2022, https://www.mckinsey.com/capabilities/strategy-and-corporate-finance/our-insights/in-conversation-four-keys-to-merger-integration-success (accessed March 25, 2025).

12. Jim Schleckser, "The Problems When Equal Companies Merge," *Inc.*, November 12, 2020, https://www.inc.com/jim-schleckser/the-problems-when-equal-companies-merge.html (accessed March 25, 2025).

13. Iskandar Aminov, Aaron De Smet, Gregor Jost, and David Mendelsohn, "Decision Making in the Age of Urgency," McKinsey & Company, April 30, 2019, https://www.mckinsey.com/capabilities/people-and-organizational-performance/our-insights/decision-making-in-the-age-of-urgency (accessed March 27, 2025); Aaron De Smet, Eileen Kelly Rinaudo, Frithjof Lund, and Leigh Weiss, "What is Decision Making?" McKinsey & Company, March 13, 2023, https://www.mckinsey.com/featured-insights/mckinsey-explainers/what-is-decision-making (accessed March 27, 2025).

14. Michael E. Porter and Nitin Nohria, "How CEOs Manage Time," *Harvard Business Review*, July 2018, https://hbr.org/2018/07/how-ceos-manage-time (accessed March 27, 2025).

15. Tim Stobierski, "The Advantages of Data-driven Decision-making," Harvard Business School online, August 26, 2019, https://online.hbs.edu/blog/post/data-driven-decision-making (accessed March 27, 2025); Tim Mucci, "What is Data-driven Decision-making?" IBM, July 23, 2024, https://www.ibm.com/think/topics/data-driven-decision-making (accessed March 27, 2025).

16. David Harding, "Writing a Credible Investment Thesis," Bain & Company, November 2004, https://www.bain.com/insights/writing-credible-investment-thesis (accessed March 26, 2025).

17. Ibid.

18. "M&A Strategy & Due Diligence," McKinsey & Company, n.d., https://www.mckinsey.com/capabilities/m-and-a/how-we-help-clients/m-and-a-strategy-due-diligence (accessed November 19, 2024).

19. Sir Andrew Likierman, "The Elements of Good Judgment," *Harvard Business Review*, January–February 2020, https://hbr.org/2020/01/the-elements-of-good-judgment (accessed March 27, 2025); Martin G. Moore, "How to Make Great Decisions, Quickly," *Harvard Business Review*, March 22, 2022, https://hbr.org/2022/03/how-to-make-great-decisions-quickly (accessed March 27, 2025).

20. Brian Contreras, "Inside Harvard's Elite Founder Class, Students Learn to Build Amid Uncertainty and AI," *Inc.*, September 3, 2025, https://www.inc.com/brian-contreras/harvard-business-school-founder-mindset-course-students-reza-satchu-uncertainty-ai/91231945 (accessed October 29, 2025).

21. Chris Isidore, "P&G to Buy Gillette for $57B," *CNN Money*, January 28, 2005, https://money.cnn.com/2005/01/28/news/fortune500/pg_gillette (accessed March 31, 2025).

22. Rosabeth Moss Kanter and Matthew Bird, "Procter & Gamble in the 21st Century (B): Welcoming Gillette," Harvard Business School case, revised September 15, 2009, 7.

23. J. Daniel Kim, "Startup Acquisitions as a Hiring Strategy: Turnover Differences Between Acquired and Regular Hires," *Strategy Science* 9, no. 2 (June 2024): 118–134. An earlier version of this article was discussed here: Meredith Somers, "Your Acquired Hires are Leaving. Here's Why," MIT Sloan, January 8, 2019, https://mitsloan.mit.edu/ideas-made-to-matter/your-acquired-hires-are-leaving-heres-why (accessed December 2, 2024).

24. "AMR Corporation and US Airways Group Come Together to Build the New American Airlines," American Airlines, press release, December 9, 2013, https://news.aa.com/news/news-details/2013/AMR-Corporation-And-US-Airways-Group-Come-Together-To-Build-The-New-American-Airlines/default.aspx (accessed April 1, 2025).

25. Daniel Jark, Jefreda Brown, and Suzanne Kvilhaug, "Understanding Financial Synergy: A Comprehensive Guide," *Investopedia*, July 26, 2024, https://www.investopedia.com/terms/s/synergy.asp (accessed April 1, 2025).

26. Oliver Engert and Rob Rosiello, "Opening the Aperture 1: A McKinsey Perspective on Value Creation and Synergies," in *Perspectives on Merger Integration* (McKinsey & Company, June 2010), 19–22, https://www.mckinsey.com/client_service/organization/latest_thinking/~/media/1002A11EEA4045899124B917EAC7404C.ashx.

27. Bernard Burnes, "The Origins of Lewin's Three-step Model of Change," *The Journal of Applied Behavioral Science* 56, no. 1 (March 2020), 32–59.

28. Jason Heinrich and Laura Miles, "Maximizing Your Merger's Potential," Bain & Company, February 2016, https://www.bain.com/insights/maximizing-your-mergers-potential (accessed March 28, 2025); McLetchie and West (2010); Scott A. Christofferson, Robert S. McNish, and Diane L. Sias, "Where Mergers Go Wrong," McKinsey & Company, May 1, 2004, https://www.mckinsey.com/capabilities/strategy-and-corporate-finance/our-insights/where-mergers-go-wrong (accessed March 28, 2025).

29. Sean Brown, Jeff Rudnicki, and Andy West, "A Winning Formula for Deal Synergies," in *Inside the Strategy Room*, McKinsey & Company, podcast, May 8, 2020, https://www.mckinsey.com/capabilities/strategy-and-corporate-finance/our-insights/a-winning-formula-for-deal-synergies (accessed April 2, 2025).

30. Mark Sirower and Jeffery Weirens, *The Synergy Solution: How Companies Win the Mergers and Acquisitions Game* (Boston, MA: Harvard Business Review Press, 2022), 198.

31. Jonathan Milde, Jacqueline Govers, Chris Barrett, and Claudio Di Vittorio, "The Critical Role of Technology and Data in Post-merger Integration," Boston Consulting Group, March 19, 2024, https://www.bcg.com/publications/2024/technologys-role-in-the-post-merger-process (accessed March 28, 2025).

32. Jeffrey Pfeffer and Robert I. Sutton, *The Knowing-Doing Gap: How Smart Companies Turn Knowledge into Action* (Boston, MA: Harvard Business School Press, 2000).

CHAPTER 2

1. Alexandra Lajoux, *The Art of M&A Integration: A Guide to Merging Resources, Processes, and Responsibilities*, second edition (New York: McGraw-Hill, 2006), 127.

2. "Utilizing an IMO (Integration Management Office)," M&A Leadership Council, October 9, 2023, https://macouncil.org/blog/2023/10/09/utilizing-imo-integration-management-office (accessed September 13, 2024).

3. David Lake and Mauro Schiavon, "Chapter 22: Integration Management Office Best Practices," in *M&A Information Technology Best Practices*, ed. Janice Roehl-Anderson (Somerset, NJ: Wiley, 2013), 393–404.

4. Satu Teerikangas and Gustavo Birollo, "Leading M&As in a Middle Managerial Role: A Balancing Act," in *Socio-Cultural Integration in Mergers and Acquisitions*, eds. Johanna Raitis, Riikka Harikkala-Laihinen, Mélanie E. Hassett, and Niina Nummela (Cham: Palgrave Pivot, 2018), 65–94.

5. Sniazhana Diduc (Sniazhko), "Integration Team Members' Approaches to Uncertainty Management in M&A," *European Management Journal* 40, no. 6 (2022): 917–931.

6. Jocelyn Chao, Oliver Engert, Ian Jefferson, Emily O'Loughlin, and Sasha Zolley, "Equipping Leaders for Merger Integration Success," McKinsey & Company, July 9, 2018, https://www.mck-insey.com/capabilities/people-and-organizational-performance/our-insights/equipping-leaders-for-merger-integration-success# (accessed April 24, 2025).
7. James McLetchie, "Next-generation Integration Management Office: A McKinsey Perspective on Organizing Integrations to Create Value," in *Perspectives on Merger Integration* (McKinsey & Company, June 2010), 31–32, https://www.mckinsey.com/client_service/organization/latest_thinking/~/media/1002A11EEA4045899124B917E-AC7404C.ashx.
8. Mitchell Lee Marks, Philip Mirvis, and Ron Ashkenas, "Surviving M&A: How to Thrive Amid the Turmoil," *Harvard Business Review*, March–April 2017, https://hbr.org/2017/03/surviving-ma (accessed July 7, 2025).
9. M&A Leadership Council (2023).

CHAPTER 3

1. "Leading in an Uncertain World," Harvard Business School Executive Education, February 12, 2019, https://www.exed.hbs.edu/blog/leadership-senior-executives-anthony-mayo (accessed February 5, 2025).
2. Ethan Bernstein, Ryan Raffaelli, and Joshua Margolis, "Leader-as-Architect: Alignment," Harvard Business School case, October 22, 2014, 1.
3. This section draws from: David G. Fubini, David A. Garvin, and Carin-Isabel Knoop, "Merging American Airlines and US Airways (A)," Harvard Business School case, revised December 4, 2017; David Fubini, Patrick Sanguineti, Carin-Isabell Knoop, and Jessica Grover, "Merging American Airlines and US Airways (A) and (B)," Harvard Business School teaching note, September 30, 2021.
4. Sniazhana Diduc (Sniazhko), "Integration Team Members' Approaches to Uncertainty Management in M&A," *European Management Journal* 40, no. 6 (2022): 921.

CHAPTER 4

1. Mark L. Sirower and Jeffery M. Weirens, *The Synergy Solution: How Companies Win the Mergers & Acquisitions Game* (Boston, MA: Harvard Business Review Press, 2022), 52.
2. Brian Boufarah and Bob Lamm, "M&A: The Intersection of Due Diligence and Governance," Deloitte, May 2016, https://www2.deloitte.com/us/en/pages/center-for-board-effective-ness/articles/mergers-and-acquisitions-due-diligence-and-governance.html.

3. Alexandra Reed Lajoux, *The Art of M&A: A Merger, Acquisition, and Buyout Guide*, sixth edition (New York: McGraw Hill, 2024), 406.
4. David Fubini, "Before a Merger, Consider Company Cultures Along with Financials," *Harvard Business Review*, December 26, 2014, https://hbr.org/2014/12/before-a-merger-consider-company-cultures-along-with-financials (accessed July 22, 2025).
5. Benjamin Farmer, Amy Wall, Emmanuel Coque, and Matthew McKenna, "The Three Most Important Steps in M&A Due Diligence," Bain & Company, September 2024, https://www.bain.com/insights/the-three-most-important-steps-in-m-and-a-due-diligence (accessed May 14, 2025).
6. Timothy Galpin and Mark Herndon, "Chapter Ten: Tracking Success Merger Measurement Systems," in *The Complete Guide to Mergers & Acquisitions: Process Tools to Support M&A Integration at Every Level*, third edition (San Francisco, CA: Josey-Bass, 2014), 259–293.
7. Mark Sirower, *The Synergy Trap: How Companies Lose the Acquisition Game* (New York: The Free Press, 1997); Mark Sirower and Sumit Sahni, "Avoiding the 'Synergy Trap': Practical Guidance on M&A Decisions for CEOs and Boards," *Journal of Applied Corporate Finance* 18, no. 3 (Summer 2006): 83–95; Mark Sirower and Jeffery Weirens, "Chapter 4: How Much Do I Need? Valuation and Synergy," in *The Synergy Solution: How Companies Win the Mergers & Acquisitions Game* (Boston, MA: Harvard Business Review Press, 2022), 89–122.
8. Sirower and Sahni (2006), 86.
9. ACSI, "American Customer Satisfaction Index Scores for Airlines in the United States from 1995 to 2025," chart, *Statista*, May 20, 2025, https://www-statista-com.ezp-prod1.hul.harvard.edu/statistics/194941/customer-satisfaction-with-us-airlines-since-1995 (accessed July 25, 2025); Harry R. Weber, "Airlines Must Work on Consumer Satisfaction," *The Royal Gazette* (Bermuda), May 15, 2007, https://www.royalgazette.com/other/business/article/20070515/airlines-must-work-on-consumer-satisfaction (accessed July 25, 2025); "18 Companies That Consumers Absolutely Hate," *Business Insider*, August 19, 2010, https://www.businessinsider.com/18-companies-that-consumers-hate-2010-8#att-mobility-1 (accessed July 25, 2025).
10. David G. Fubini, David A. Garvin, and Carin-Isabel Knoop, "Merging American Airlines and US Airways (A)," Harvard Business School case, revised December 4, 2017, 3.
11. Adam Haller, Benjamin Farmer, and Suzanne Kumar, "Bringing Science to the Art of Revenue Synergies," Bain & Company, February 2022, https://www.bain.com/insights/revenue-synergies-m-and-a-report-2022 (accessed July 28, 2025); Khalid Khan and Derron Stark, "Three Ways a Data Clean Room Can Help You Realized M&A Synergies Faster," EY, March 3, 2022, https://www.ey.com/en_us/insights/mergers-acquisitions/how-to-realize-synergies-sooner-with-a-clean-room (accessed August 19, 2024).
12. Rosabeth Moss Kanter and Matthew Bird, "Procter & Gamble in the 21st Century (B): Welcoming Gillette," Harvard Business School case, revised September 15, 2009, 9.

13. Lajoux (2024), 27–30.
14. Lawrence Siff, "The 7 Deadly Sins of Mergers and Acquisitions," *Forbes* online, August 20, 2012, https://www.forbes.com/sites/lawrencesiff/2012/08/20/the-7-deadly-sins-of-mergers-and-acquisitions (accessed August 28, 2024); Lajoux (2024), 25–26; "How Can SWOT Analysis Improve Your Mergers and Acquisitions Strategy?" LinkedIn, community blog post, December 30, 2023, https://www.linkedin.com/advice/0/how-can-swot-analysis-improve-your-mergers-acquisitions-g0gpf (accessed August 28, 2024). A Harvard Business Review classic provides the essentials of what you need to know in using this analysis internally for your business and tying it to strategy development: Richard Luecke, *Harvard Business Essentials: Strategy: Create and Implement the Best Strategy for Your Business* (Boston, MA: Harvard Business School Press, 2005).
15. Oliver Engert, Max Flötotto, Greg Gryzwa, Milind Sachdeva, and Patryk Strojny, "Eight Basic Beliefs About Capturing Value in a Merger," McKinsey & Company, April 2, 2019, https://www.mckinsey.com/capabilities/people-and-organizational-performance/our-insights/eight-basic-beliefs-about-capturing-value-in-a-merger (accessed July 28, 2025).
16. Scott C. Whitaker, "Chapter 8: Executing Your Integration Plan," in *Mergers & Acquisitions Integration Handbook* (Hoboken, NJ: Wiley, 2012), 75–85.
17. Daniel Friedman, Axel Reinaud, Chris Barrett, and Niamh Dawson, "Six Essentials for Achieving Postmerger Synergies," Boston Consulting Group, March 17, 2017, https://www.bcg.com/publications/2017/postmerger-integration-six-essentials-for-achieving-postmerger-synergies (accessed April 23, 2025).

CHAPTER 5

1. Bronwyn Fryer, "Storytelling That Moves People," *Harvard Business Magazine*, June 2003, https://hbr.org/2003/06/storytelling-that-moves-people (accessed February 4, 2025).
2. Jennifer Aaker, "Harnessing the Power of Stories," Stanford VMware Women's Leadership Innovation Lab, n.d., https://womensleadership.stanford.edu/node/796/harnessing-power-stories (accessed February 4, 2025).
3. Vanessa Boris, "What Makes Storytelling So Effective for Learning?" Harvard Business Publishing Corporate Learning, December 20, 2017, https://www.harvardbusiness.org/what-makes-storytelling-so-effective-for-learning (accessed February 4, 2025).
4. Lani Peterson, "The Science Behind the Art of Storytelling," Harvard Business Publishing Corporate Learning, November 14, 2017, https://www.harvardbusiness.org/the-science-behind-the-art-of-storytelling (accessed February 4, 2025).

5. Paul A. Argenti, Robert A. Howell, and Karen A. Beck, "The Strategic Communication Imperative," *MIT Sloan Management Review*, April 15, 2005, https://sloanreview.mit.edu/article/the-strategic-communication-imperative (accessed January 14, 2025).

6. Ibid.

7. Constantinos C. Markides and Andrew MacLennan, "3 Ways to Clearly Communicate Your Company's Strategy," *Harvard Business Review*, May 24, 2024, https://hbr.org/2024/05/3-ways-to-clearly-communicate-your-companys-strategy (accessed January 14, 2025).

8. Donald Sull, Stefano Turconi, Charles Sull, and James Yoder, "Turning Strategy into Results," *MIT Sloan Management Review*, September 28, 2017, https://sloanreview.mit.edu/article/turning-strategy-into-results (accessed January 14, 2025); Donald Sull, Charles Sull, and James Yoder, "No One Knows Your Strategy—Not Even Your Top Leaders," *MIT Sloan Management Review*, February 12, 2018, https://sloanreview.mit.edu/article/no-one-knows-your-strategy-not-even-your-top-leaders (accessed January 14, 2025).

9. Fernando Suarez and Gianvito Lanzolla, "The Half-Truth of First-Mover Advantage," *Harvard Business Review*, April 2005, https://hbr.org/2005/04/the-half-truth-of-first-mover-advantage (accessed March 21, 2025).

10. Jerome Bruner, "The Narrative Construction of Reality," *Critical Inquiry* 18, no. 1 (Autum 1991): 18–20.

11. Amos Tversky and Daniel Kahneman, "Judgment under Uncertainty: Heuristics and Biases," *Science* 185, no. 4157 (1974): 1124–1131. For a concise summary, see: "What is the Anchoring Effect?" Harvard Law School Program on Negotiation, n.d., https://www.pon.harvard.edu/tag/the-anchoring-effect (accessed March 21, 2025).

12. Bill Stephens, "Canadian Pacific, Kansas City Southern Merger to Redraw Class I Railroad Map," Trains.com, March 21, 2021, https://www.trains.com/trn/canadian-pacific-kansas-city-southern-merger-to-redraw-class-i-railroad-map (accessed April 3, 2025); Niraj Chokshi and Mark Walker, "U.S. Approves $31 Billion Merger of Two Big Railroads," *The New York Times*, March 15, 2023, https://www.nytimes.com/2023/03/15/business/canadian-pacific-kansas-city-southern-merger.html (accessed April 3, 2025).

13. "Canadian Pacific and Kansas City Southern Execute Agreement to Combine, Creating First Single-Line Rail Network Linking U.S.-Mexico-Canada," Canadian Pacific Kansas City Southern, press release, September 15, 2021, https://investor.cpkcr.com/news/press-release-details/2021/Canadian-Pacific-and-Kansas-City-Southern-Execute-Agreement-to-Combine-Creating-First-Single-Line-Rail-Network-Linking-U.S.-Mexico-Canada/default.aspx (accessed April 3, 2025).

14. Karl E. Weick, Kathleen M. Sutcliffe, and David Obstfeld, "Organizing and the Process of Sensemaking," *Organization Science* 16, no. 4 (2005): 409–419.

15. Rosabeth Moss Kanter and Matthew Bird, "Procter & Gamble in the 21st Century (B): Welcoming Gillette," Harvard Business School case, revised September 15, 2009, 7–8.

16. Dennis Carey, "Lessons from Master Acquirers: A CEO Roundtable on Making Mergers Succeed," *Harvard Business Review*, May–June 2000, 152.
17. Spencer Soper and Olivia Zaleski, "Inside Amazon's Battle to Break into the $800 Billion Grocery Market," *Bloomberg* online, March 20, 2017, https://www.bloomberg. com/news/features/2017-03-20/inside-amazon-s-battle-to-break-into-the-800-billion-grocery-market (accessed January 28, 2025).
18. Jose B. Alvarez, David Lane, and Joni Coughlin, "Amazon Buys Whole Foods," Harvard Business School case, revised May 30, 2018, 11.
19. Hamid Bouchikhi and John R. Kimberly, "Making Mergers Work," *MIT Sloan Management Review* 54, no. 1 (Fall 2012): 63–70.
20. "Microsoft to Acquire LinkedIn," Microsoft, press release, June 13, 2016, https://news.microsoft.com/2016/06/13/microsoft-to-acquire-linkedin (accessed January 28, 2025).
21. Ibid.
22. "Amazon to Acquire Whole Foods Market," Whole Foods, press release, June 16, 2017, https://media.wholefoodsmarket.com/amazon-to-acquire-whole-foods-market (accessed January 29, 2025).
23. Norbert Steigenberger, "The Challenge of Integration: A Review of the M&A Integration Literature," *International Journal of Management Reviews* 19, no. 4 (2017): 417–419.
24. J. Daniel Kim, "Startup Acquisitions as a Hiring Strategy: Turnover Differences Between Acquired and Regular Hires," *Strategy Science* 9, no. 2 (June 2024): 118–134.
25. For example: Kristine Coogan, Satiya Witzer, and Bobby Berkowitz, "Talent Flight: Overlooked Risks During M&A," KPMG, 2023, https://kpmg.com/kpmg-us/content/dam/kpmg/pdf/2023/talent-flight-overlooked-risks-during-m-a.pdf (accessed January 29, 2025); "2024 M&A Retention Study," WTW, March 13, 2024, https://www.wtwco.com/en-us/insights/2024/03/2024-m-and-a-retention-study (accessed January 29, 2025); Mark Carroll and Andy Rowsell-Jones, "Retain Key Employees to Gain in M&A," Gartner, August 8, 2024, https://www.gartner.com/en/documents/5658723 (accessed January 29, 2025); Edmund Tirbutt, "How to Retain Staff During Mergers and Acquisitions," *HR Magazine* online, December 16, 2024, https://www.hrmagazine.co.uk/content/features/how-to-retain-staff-during-mergers-and-acquisitions (accessed January 29, 2025).
26. Rudolf R. Sinkovics, Stefan Zagelmeyer, and Verena Kusstatscher, "Between Merger and Syndrome: The Intermediary Role of Emotions in Four Cross-border M&As," *International Business Review* 20, no. 1 (2011): 27–47. The term was popularized by: Philip Mirvis and Mitchell Lee Marks, "Merger Syndrome: Stress and Uncertainty," *Mergers & Acquisitions* 20, no. 2 (July 1985), 50; Philip Mirvis and Mitchell Lee Marks, "Merger Syndrome: Management by Crisis," *Mergers & Acquisitions* 20, no. 3 (January/ February 1986): 70–76.

27. Dina Bass and Brian Womack, "Dell Technologies to Cut at Least 2,000 Jobs After EMC Deal," *Bloomberg* online, September 8, 2016, https://www.bloomberg.com/news/articles/2016-09-08/dell-technologies-said-to-cut-at-least-2-000-jobs-after-emc-deal (accessed January 29, 2025).

28. Glenda McCarthy, "Hewlett-Packard to Cut 1,800 More Jobs," *Los Angeles Times*, September 26, 2002, https://www.latimes.com/archives/la-xpm-2002-sep-26-fi-hp26-story.html (accessed January 29, 2025); Pui-Wing Tam, "H-P to Lay Off More Workers in the Wake of Compaq Deal," *The Wall Street Journal*, September 26, 2002, https://www.wsj.com/articles/SB103297191436283753 (accessed January 29, 2025).

29. Ed O'Boyle and Amy Adkins, "Often Overlooked in M&A: Customers and Employees," Gallup, November 24, 2015, https://news.gallup.com/business journal/186875/often-overlooked-customers-employees.aspx (accessed January 31, 2025).

30. Kanter and Bird (2009), 2.

31. *People Risks in M&A Transactions* (Mercer, 2016), 35, https://www.marshmclennan.com/web-assets/insights/publications/2020/october/gl-mergers-and-acquisitions-people-risks-report-mercer.pdf.

32. This paragraph, including the quotation from Moheet Nagrath, is adapted from Kanter and Bird (2009), 7.

33. Rosabeth Moss Kanter, "Five Tips for Coping with Uncertainty and Finding Opportunity," *Harvard Business Review*, July 25, 2011, https://hbr.org/2011/07/five-tips-for-coping-with-unce (accessed February 3, 2025).

34. Duncan Angwin, Kamel Mellahi, Emanuel Gomes, and Emmanuel Peter, "How Communication Approaches Impact Mergers and Acquisitions Outcomes," *The International Journal of Human Resource Management* (December 2014): 2370–2397, https://doi.org/10.1080/09585192.2014.985330.

35. Sinkovics et al. (2011), 39.

36. Angwin et al. (2014).

CHAPTER 6

1. "Udemy Expands Industry-Leading Creative Capabilities with Addition of Lummi's AI-Powered Design Tools," Business Wire, press release, June 18, 2025, https://www.businesswire.com/news/home/20250618180355/en/Udemy-Expands-Industry-Leading-Creative-Capabilities-with-Addition-of-Lummis-AI-Powered-Design-Tools (accessed June 23, 2025).

2. "Kering Eyewear Acquires Italian Manufacturer Lenti," Kering, press release, June 10, 2025, https://www.kering.com/en/news/kering-eyewear-acquires-italian-manufacturer-lenti (accessed June 23, 2025).

3. "Aya Healthcare Acquires Locum's Nest to Advance Innovative Workforce Solutions in the UK," Business Wire, press release, June 20, 2025, https://www.businesswire.com/news/home/20250620266173/en/Aya-Healthcare-Acquires-Locums-Nest-to-Advance-Innovative-Workforce-Solutions-in-the-UK (accessed June 23, 2025).

4. Mark Sirower and Jeffery Weirens, *The Synergy Solution: How Companies Win in the Mergers & Acquisitions Game* (Boston, MA: Harvard Business Review Press, 2022), 218.

5. David Fubini, Colin Price, and Maurizio Zollo, *Mergers: Leadership, Performance and Corporate Health* (New York: Palgrave MacMillan, 2007), 16.

6. Even if not strictly "equal," in the past, many deals that tried to avoid the perception of a takeover have agreed to a combined board, the makeup of which often reflects the balance of power between the two sides: Alexandra Reed Lajoux, *The Art of M&A Integration: A Guide to Merging Resources, Processes, and Responsibilities*, second edition (New York: McGraw-Hill, 2006), 119–120.

7. Randel S. Carlock and Elizabeth Florent-Treacy, "The HP-Compaq Merger: A Battle for the Heart and Soul of a Company (A)," INSEAD, revised 2006, https://hbsp.harvard.edu/product/INS408-PDF-ENG?Ntt=HP%20compaq.

8. David Fubini, Patrick Sanguineti, Carin-Isabell Knoop, and Jessica Grover, "Merging American Airlines and US Airways (A) and (B)," Harvard Business School teaching note, September 30, 2021, 9.

9. Adam Haller and Scott Nancarrow, "The 10 Steps to Successful M&A Integration," Bain & Company, June 2024, https://www.bain.com/insights/10-steps-to-successful-ma-integration (accessed July 16, 2025).

10. Robert Werner, Henning Streubel, Deborah Lovich, and Joseph Halverson, "When Leaders Say They are Aligned—but Aren't," Boston Consulting Group, December 8, 2021, https://www.bcg.com/publications/2021/when-leadership-say-they-are-aligned-but-company-leaders-are-not (accessed May 15, 2025).

11. Sirower and Weirens (2022), 191–197, provides a more granular description of these two approaches to talent selection.

12. Brian Dinneen, Christine Johnson, Becky Kaetzler, and Alex Liu, "In Conversation: Four Keys to Merger Integration Success," McKinsey & Company, October 12, 2022, https://www.mckinsey.com/capabilities/strategy-and-corporate-finance/our-insights/in-conversation-four-keys-to-merger-integration-success (accessed September 9, 2024).

13. Judith Kimerling, "Lessons from the Chevron Ecuador Litigation: The Proposed Intervenors' Perspective," *Stanford Journal of Complex Litigation* 1, no. 2 (Spring 2013): 241–294; Lorenzo Pellegrini, Murat Arsel, Martí Orta-Martínez, and Carlos F. Mena, "International Investment Agreements, Human Rights, and Environmental Justice: The Texaco/Chevron Case from the Ecuadorian Amazon," *Journal of Economic Law* 23, no. 2 (June 2020): 455–468; Paul Paz y Miño, "Chevron's Environmental Crimes: 13 Years of Evasion and Escalation," Amazon Watch, February 14, 2024, https://

amazonwatch.org/news/2024/0214-chevrons-environmental-crimes-13-years-of-evasion-and-escalation (accessed February 14, 2025).

14. Barry Meier and Andrew Ross Sorkin, "Guidant Sues Johnson & Johnson for Completion of Merger," *The New York Times*, November 8, 2005, https://www.nytimes.com/2005/11/08/business/guidant-sues-johnson-johnson-for-completion-of-merger.html (accessed February 14, 2025); David Gelles, "Boston Scientific and J.&J. Settle Suit Over Guidant Deal," *The New York Times*, February 17, 2015, https://archive.nytimes.com/dealbook.nytimes.com/2015/02/17/boston-scientific-and-jj-settle-suit-over-guidant-deal (accessed February 14, 2025).

15. "Medical Device Manufacturer Guidant Charged in Failure to Report Defibrillator Safety Problems to FDA," U.S. Department of Justice, press release, February 25, 2010, https://www.justice.gov/archives/opa/pr/medical-device-manufacturer-guidant-charged-failure-report-defibrillator-safety-problems-fda (accessed February 14, 2025).

16. For example, Universal Studios employees were startled to find their email addresses suddenly changed without warning after its acquisition by NBC: Brooks Barnes, "Disney and Pixar: The Power of the Prenup," *The New York Times*, June 1, 2008, https://www.nytimes.com/2008/06/01/business/media/01pixar.html (accessed July 15, 2025).

17. ESPN.com Staff, "The Wizard's Wisdom: 'Woodensisms.'" ESPN, June 4, 2010, https://www.espn.com/mens-college-basketball/news/story?id=5249709 (accessed October 28, 2025).

CHAPTER 7

1. Rita Zinn, "The First 100 Days: A Blueprint for M&A Integration Success," Pioneer Management Consulting, August 22, 2023, https://www.pioneer managementconsulting.com/insights/the-first-100-days-a-blueprint-for-ma-integration-success (accessed July 10, 2025).

2. Niki St. Pierre, "'Change' Communication in Post-M&A Integration: The First 100 Days," Catalant, May 13, 2024, https://catalant.com/business-agility/change-communication-in-post-integration-the-first-100-days (accessed July 10, 2025).

3. Christoph Stich and Igor Barkalov, "The First 100 Days," Capgemini Consulting, 2016, https://www.eprentise.com/wp-content/uploads/capgemini-first-100-days-merger.pdf (accessed July 10, 2025).

4. Duncan Angwin, "Speed in M&A Integration: The First 100 Days," *European Management Journal* 22, no. 4 (2004): 418–430.

5. Mark Thomas, Duncan Angwin, Ioannis Thanos, Gazi Islam, and Robert Demir, "Speeds of Post-merger Integration: The Roles of *Chronos* and *Kairos* in M&As," *Long Range Planning* 56, no. 6 (2023): 2, https://doi.org/10.1016/j.lrp.2023.102345.

6. Eileen Fernandez, Tom Joseph, Davi Bryan, and Matt Usdin, "People-related 'Must Do's' for the First 100 Days," Deloitte, 2017, https://www2.deloitte.com/content/dam/Deloitte/us/Documents/mergers-acqisitions/us-ma-people-related-must-dos-for-the-first-hundred-days.pdf (accessed September 3, 2024); Cheryl Meyer, "Crafting a 100-day M&A Integration Road Map," *Financial Management* online, February 1, 2020, https://www.fm-magazine.com/issues/2020/feb/100-day-post-merger-integration-road-map.html (accessed September 3, 2024).

7. Brian Dinneen, Christine Johnson, and Alex Liu, "Post-close Excellence in Large-deal M&A," McKinsey & Company, June 29, 2021, https://www.mckinsey.com/capabilities/m-and-a/our-insights/post-close-excellence-in-large-deal-m-and-a (accessed October 21, 2025).

8. ESPN.com Staff, "The Wizard's Wisdom: 'Woodensisms.'" ESPN, June 4, 2010, https://www.espn.com/mens-college-basketball/news/story?id=5249709 (accessed October 28, 2025).

9. Timothy Galpin and Mark Herndon, "Merger Repair: When M&As Go Wrong," *The Journal of Business Strategy* 29, no. 1 (2008): 4–12; Timothy Galpin and Mark Herndon, "Chapter 13: Merger Repair," in *The Complete Guide to Mergers & Acquisitions*, third edition (San Francisco, CA: Jossey-Bass, 2014), 331–346.

CHAPTER 8

1. Oliver Engert, Becky Kaetzler, Kameron Kordestani, and Andy MacLean, "Organizational Culture in Mergers: Addressing the Unseen Forces," McKinsey & Company, March 26, 2019, https://www.mckinsey.com/capabilities/people-and-organizational-performance/our-insights/organizational-culture-in-mergers-addressing-the-unseen-forces (accessed October 2, 2024).

2. Jocelyn Chao, Rebecca Kaetzler, Kameron Kordestani, and Emily O'Louglin, "The Culture Compass: Using Early Insights to Guide Integration Planning," McKinsey & Company, February 29, 2024, https://www.mckinsey.com/capabilities/m-and-a/our-insights/the-culture-compass-using-early-insights-to-guide-integration-planning (accessed September 13, 2024).

3. Erin Gillman, Sinead Mullen, Scott Nancarrow, and Marc Berman, "How to Avoid the Fault Lines Sending Tremors Through Cultural Integration in M&A," Bain & Company, January 2023, https://www.bain.com/insights/cultural-integration-m-and-a-report-2023 (accessed August 27, 2025).

4. Boris Groysberg, Jeremiah Lee, Jesse Price, and J. Yo-Jud Cheng, "The Leader's Guide to Corporate Culture," *Harvard Business Review*, January–February 2018, https://hbr.org/2018/01/the-leaders-guide-to-corporate-culture (accessed August 11, 2025).

5. Edgar Schein first discussed "visible artifacts," the perceptible markers of organizational culture, in: "Coming to a New Awareness of Organizational Culture," *MIT Sloan Management Review* 25, no. 2 (Winter 1984): 3–16.
6. D. D. Warrick, "What Leaders Need to Know about Organizational Culture," *Business Horizons* 60, no. 3 (2017): 395–404.
7. Edgar Schein, *Organizational Culture and Leadership*, fifth edition (Hoboken, NJ: Wiley, 1985 [2017]). For a brief summary, see: Meredith Somers, "5 Enduring Management Ideas from MIT Sloan's Edgar Schein," MIT Sloan, February 9, 2023, https://mitsloan.mit.edu/ideas-made-to-matter/5-enduring-management-ideas-mit-sloans-edgar-schein (accessed October 3, 2024).
8. Ram Charan, "Home Depot's Blueprint for Culture Change," *Harvard Business Review*, April 2006, https://hbr.org/2006/04/home-depots-blueprint-for-culture-change (accessed October 2, 2024).
9. Chris Barrett, Daniel Friedman, Jim Hemerling, and Julie Kilmann, "Breaking the Cultural Barrier in Postmerger Integrations," Boston Consulting Group, January 13, 2016, https://www.bcg.com/publications/2016/breaking-the-culture-barrier-in-postmerger-integrations (accessed October 2, 2024).
10. John Shook, "How to Change a Culture: Lessons from NUMMI," *MIT Sloan Management Review* 51, no. 2 (Winter 2010): 63–68.
11. Jocelyn Chao, Oliver Engert, Ian Jefferson, Emily O'Loughlin, and Sasha Zolley, "Equipping Leaders for Merger Integration Success," McKinsey & Company, July 9, 2018, https://www.mckinsey.com/capabilities/people-and-organizational-performance/our-insights/equipping-leaders-for-merger-integration-success# (accessed August 27, 2025).
12. The following vignette is adapted from: Rosabeth Moss Kanter and Matthew Bird, "Procter & Gamble in the 21st Century (A): Becoming Truly Global," Harvard Business School case, revised September 15, 2009; "Procter & Gamble in the 21st Century (B): Welcoming Gillette," Harvard Business School case, revised September 15, 2009; "Procter & Gamble in the 21st Century (C): Integrating Gillette," Harvard Business School case, revised September 15, 2009.
13. Kanter and Bird (2009), "Procter & Gamble (B)," 10.
14. Ibid., 11.
15. "James M. Kilts, '74." Chicago Booth, n.d., https://www.chicagobooth.edu/alumni/distinguished-alumni-award/honorees/james-kilts (accessed October 30, 2024).
16. Kanter and Bird (2009), "Procter & Gamble (B)," 11.
17. Kanter and Bird (2009), "Procter & Gamble (C)," 6–7.
18. Todd Corley, Vontrese (Voni) Pamphile, and Katina Sawyer, "What Has (and Hasn't) Changed about Being a Chief Diversity Officer," *Harvard Business Review*, September 23, 2022, https://hbr.org/2022/09/what-has-and-hasnt-changed-about-being-a-chief-diversity-officer (accessed August 12, 2025).
19. Kanter and Bird (2009), "Procter & Gamble (B)," 8; "Procter & Gamble (C)," 6.
20. Gillman et al. (2023).

21. Bernard Burnes, "The Origins of Lewin's Three-step Model of Change," *The Journal of Applied Behavioral Science* 56, no. 1 (March 2020): 32–59.

22. John Kotter, "Leading Change: Why Transformation Efforts Fail," in *HBR's 10 Must Reads: On Change Management* (Boston, MA: Harvard Business School Publishing Corporation, 2011), 1–16.

23. Ignacio Fantaguzzi and Christopher Handscomb, "The Importance of Cultural Integration in M&A: The Path to Success," McKinsey &Company, February 1, 2024, https://www.mckinsey.com/industries/oil-and-gas/our-insights/the-importance-of-cultural-integration-in-m-and-a-the-path-to-success (accessed October 2, 2024).

24. Gillman et al. (2023).

25. John Kotter, Vanessa Akhtar, and Gaurav Gupta, *Change: How Organizations Achieve Hard-to-Imagine Results in Uncertain and Volatile Times* (Hoboken, NJ: Wiley, 2021), 135.

26. Fantaguzzi and Handscomb (2024).

27. John Kotter, Vanessa Akhtar, and Gaurav Gupta, "Overcoming Obstacles to Successful Culture Change," *MIT Sloan Management Review*, July 2021, https://sloanreview.mit.edu/article/overcoming-obstacles-to-successful-culture-change (accessed October 2, 2024).

28. Kotter et al. (2021), "Overcoming Obstacles to Successful Cultural Change." See also: Bryan Walker and Sarah A. Soule, "Changing Company Culture Requires a Movement, Not a Mandate," *Harvard Business Review*, June 20, 2017, https://hbr.org/2017/06/changing-company-culture-requires-a-movement-not-a-mandate (accessed October 2, 2024).

29. Sigal Barsade, "Five Steps for Managing Culture Change," Wharton Executive Education, *Wharton@Work* (blog), September 2014, https://executiveeducation.wharton.upenn.edu/thought-leadership/wharton-at-work/2014/09/managing-culture-change (accessed October 2, 2024).

30. Kotter et al. (2021), *Change*, 118.

31. The following draws from: David G. Fubini and Christine Snively, "Lenovo to Buy IBM PC: Integration Challenges," Harvard Business School case, revised July 1, 2019; Aijing Ran, Xiaobing Liu, Jiawei Dong, Yuekun Liu, and Miao Cui, "Lenovo: Is the Cultural Integration Template Reusable?" Ivey School of Business case, December 22, 2016; William J. Holstein, "Lenovo Goes Global," Strategy+Business, August 8, 2014, https://www.strategy-business.com/article/00274 (accessed September 15, 2025).

32. Ran et al. (2016), 7.

33. Tim Bajarin, "10 Years Later, Looking Back at the IBM-Lenovo PC Deal," *PCMag* online, May 4, 2015, https://www.pcmag.com/opinions/10-years-later-looking-back-at-the-ibm-lenovo-pc-deal (accessed September 15, 2025).

34. Janessa Rivera, "Gartner Says Worldwide PC Shipments Declined 6.9 Percent in Fourth Quarter of 2013," Gartner, January 9, 2014, https://web.archive.org/web/20140110052948/ http://www.gartner.com/newsroom/id/2647517 (accessed September 15, 2025).
35. The following draws from: David G. Fubini, Rawi Abdelal, and David Lane, "Integrating Beam Suntory (A)," Harvard Business School case, revised February 2, 2021; "Integrating Beam Suntory (B)," Harvard Business School case, revised November 13, 2020.

CHAPTER 9

1. Mark L. Sirower and Jeffery M. Weirens, *The Synergy Solution: How Companies Win the Mergers & Acquisitions Game* (Boston, MA: Harvard Business Review Press, 2022), 224.
2. Ibid., 227–228. See also: Scott C. Whitaker, *Mergers & Acquisitions Integration Handbook* (Hoboken, NJ: Wiley, 2012), 87–93.
3. Timothy Galpin and Mark Herndon, *The Complete Guide to Mergers & Acquisitions: Process Tools to Support M&A Integration at Every Level*, third edition (San Francisco, CA: Jossey-Bass, 2014), 347.
4. Jennifer Fondrevay, "M&A Should Be Transformation – Not Transactional," *Harvard Business Review*, May 29, 2024, https://hbr.org/2024/05/ma-should-be-transformational-not-transactional (accessed September 9, 2024).
5. Scott C. Whitaker, "Chapter 15: Integration Feedback: Lessons Learned" and "Chapter 16: Creating an Integration Playbook," in *Mergers & Acquisitions Integration Handbook* (Hoboken, NJ: Wiley, 2012), 149–162.
6. Ronald N. Ashkenas, Lawrence J. DeMonaco, and Suzanne C. Francis, "Making the Deal Real: How GE Capital Integrates Acquisitions," *Harvard Business Review*, January–February 1998, https://hbr.org/1998/01/making-the-deal-real-how-ge-capital-integrates-acquisitions (accessed July 7, 2025).
7. "Monitor Deloitte's 2025 Chief Transformation Officer Study," Deloitte, 2025, https://www.deloitte.com/content/dam/assets-zone3/us/en/docs/services/consulting/2025/us-2025-chief-transformation-officer-survey.pdf (accessed July 7, 2025).
8. Mitchell Lee Marks, Philip Mirvis, and Ron Ashkenas, "Surviving M&A: How to Thrive Amid the Turmoil," *Harvard Business Review*, March–April 2017, https://hbr.org/2017/03/surviving-ma (accessed July 7, 2025).
9. Kurt Chauviere, Ben Maritz, and Jasper van Halder, "The Role of the Transformation Office," McKinsey & Company, November 17, 2016, https://www.mckinsey.com/capabilities/rts/our-insights/the-role-of-the-transformation-office# (accessed June 30, 2025).

INDEX

Note: Page numbers in *italics* refer to figures.